The Hidden History
of Monopolies

THE

HIDDEN HISTORY *of*

MONOPOLIES

—————— HOW ——————

BIG BUSINESS DESTROYED
the AMERICAN DREAM

THOM HARTMANN

BK

Berrett–Koehler Publishers, Inc.

Berrett-Koehler Publishers, Inc.
1333 Broadway, Suite 1000
Oakland, CA 94612-1921
Tel: (510) 817-2277
Fax: (510) 817-2278
www.bkconnection.com

ORDERING INFORMATION

Quantity sales. Special discounts are available on quantity purchases by corporations, associations, and others. For details, contact the "Special Sales Department" at the Berrett-Koehler address above.

Individual sales. Berrett-Koehler publications are available through most bookstores. They can also be ordered directly from Berrett-Koehler: Tel: (800) 929-2929; Fax: (802) 864-7626; www.bkconnection.com.

Orders for college textbook / course adoption use. Please contact Berrett-Koehler: Tel: (800) 929-2929; Fax: (802) 864-7626.

Distributed to the U.S. trade and internationally by Penguin Random House Publisher Services.

Berrett-Koehler and the BK logo are registered trademarks of Berrett-Koehler Publishers, Inc.

Printed in the United States of America

Berrett-Koehler books are printed on long-lasting acid-free paper. When it is available, we choose paper that has been manufactured by environmentally responsible processes. These may include using trees grown in sustainable forests, incorporating recycled paper, minimizing chlorine in bleaching, or recycling the energy produced at the paper mill.

Library of Congress Cataloging-in-Publication Data
Names: Hartmann, Thom, 1951– author.
Title: The hidden history of monopolies : how big business destroyed the
   American dream / Thom Hartmann.
Description: First Edition. | Oakland : Berrett-Koehler Publishers, 2020. |
   Series: The Thom Hartmann hidden history series; 4 | Includes
   bibliographical references and index.
Identifiers: LCCN 2020008983 | ISBN 9781523087730 (paperback) | ISBN
   9781523087747 (pdf) | ISBN 9781523087754 (epub)
Subjects: LCSH: Monopolies—United States—History. |
   Monopolies—Government policy—United States. | Mass media—Economic
   aspects—United States. | Antitrust law—United States.
Classification: LCC HD2757.2 .H37 2020 | DDC 338.8/20973—dc23
LC record available at https://lccn.loc.gov/2020008983

First Edition
28 27 26 25 24 23 22 21   10 9 8 7 6 5 4 3

Book production: Linda Jupiter Productions; *Cover design:* Wes Youssi, M.80 Design;
Edit: Elissa Rabellino; *Proofread:* Mary Kanable; *Index:* Paula C. Durbin-Westby

*The American Beauty rose can be produced
in the splendor and fragrance which bring cheer to its beholder
only by sacrificing the early buds which grow up around it.
This is not an evil tendency in business.
It is merely the working-out of a law of nature
and a law of God.*
—John D. Rockefeller

CONTENTS

FOREWORD

By Ralph Nader

This is the most important, dynamic book—small as it is—on the cancers of monopoly by giant corporations written in our generation. I have read many books on monopolistic practices and have written on this subject. None had the potential to reach the moral imagination and indignation of the American people, where they live, work, and raise their families, like Hartmann's engrossing volume. None, for sure, had the potential to reach so many members of Congress who are finally awakening to the long-overdue accounting of monopoly's many costs—economic and beyond economic—and the need to strengthen the old antitrust laws and enact the new ones that reach all the way to Silicon Valley.

Because he has for many years had a daily three-hour national radio talk show, Hartmann knows how to communicate importance to everyone, regardless of their self-described political persuasions. Because he is by far the most erudite longtime national radio talk show host, he has had an uncanny sense of retrieving critical segments of American history, ignored by historians, regarding the suspicion and caution our forebears had about this artificial entity called the large corporation as it became more immune and more privileged than real human beings.

It was Hartmann, a prolific published historian, who dug out the records surrounding the notorious 1886 Supreme Court case *Santa Clara County v. Southern Pacific Railroad Co.*, where the scribe—formerly a railroad man—distorted the decision in his case summary to say that all corporations are "persons" for purposes of the 14th Amendment to our Constitution. It was Hartmann who rescued from history the heroic efforts by our forebears to stop the ravaging structures of corporations, enabled by their corporate lawyers who wrote the very corporate laws allowing their clients to become lawlessly "lawful" before the lobbyists rammed them through state legislatures and Congress.

From the time in the 19th century when state legislatures held these corporations under charters that required renewal and even embraced a "corporate death penalty," which Hartmann describes, giant corporatism has steadily imposed its corporate supremacy—profit at any cost—over workers; consumers; communities; small taxpayers; public budgets; and, most crucially, the local, state, and national governments of our country. Relentlessly, there looms an ever-deeper corporate state—what President Franklin Delano Roosevelt called "fascism" in his 1938 message to Congress proposing a commission to investigate corporate power that also seized government power.

Today, giant corporatism—the commercialism of just about everything at the expense of our civilization's civic, spiritual, health, and safety values, and other conditions needed for the well-being of future generations confronting poverty, addressing planetary climate crises, and averting nuclear war—is crushing our democracy. It is corrupting our elections and, astonishingly enough, controlling the vast *commons*—public lands; public airwaves; vast pension and mutual funds; and industry-creating, government-funded research and development—*owned* by the people.

We plan to see that Hartmann's book is required reading by as many members of Congress as possible. You can galvanize its messages through discussion groups, library meetings, school adoptions, and simply talking it up with your circle of friends, neighbors, coworkers, and reporters.

Maybe you think the subject of monopoly is too legalistic or arcane. Start reading and see how many times you say "ouch" to yourself and perhaps decide to put this book on wheels for civic and government action. We need to rewrite the existing monopoly rules and enable quality competition and alert civic voice to shape a just and productive political economy.

An ancient Roman adage is pertinent: "What touches all must be approved by all."

Ralph Nader
Washington, DC

Cancer and Monopoly

Cell phone service that costs $15 a month in France or $12 a month in Australia bills out at an average of $61.85 per month in the United States. High-speed broadband that's a bit over $31 a month in France or $36 in Germany (for higher speeds and better reliability than almost anywhere in the United States) averages nearly $70 per month in the US. Similar metrics are found with pharmaceuticals, airfares, and medical costs, among dozens of other product and service categories.[1]

Why is this? Monopoly.

The average American family pays an annual "monopoly tax"—in additional costs for pretty much everything—of around $5,000, according to economist Thomas Philippon. And things are steadily getting worse as monopolistic concentrations continue to tighten their grip on every American industry from banking to telecom to food.[2]

Monopoly isn't the arcane, legalistic thing that most Americans think of (if they're not mistaking it for the board game, which was invented by Elizabeth Magie in 1904 as a cautionary tale[3]). In multiple very real ways, monopoly touches the lives of all of us.

A *monopoly* is broadly defined as a single part of a larger system that takes over or dominates, controls, and consumes all the energy and functions of the entire system. In the process, the system is warped and twisted away from its normal function and, like a body reacting to a cancer, begins to redirect all its resources to feed the single monopolistic entity.

Cancer in the body works pretty much the same way that monopoly works across an entire spectrum of things, from monopolies in business to monopolies in religion, language, agriculture, power systems, and, ultimately, the biological systems of the planet over which we humans have seized monopoly control.

This book is about what happens when the cancer of monopoly infects the economic, political, religious, atmospheric, biospheric, or cultural body. In virtually every regard, the explosion of humanity across our planet, along with our monopolization of the food, water, soil, and cultural resources of the planet, is cancer-like. Big business has done the same in our economic and political realms. The result—if we don't get this under control soon—will be disaster.

Which raises a fundamental question, asked from the days of Plato to Adam Smith to Bernie Sanders: Is the economy here to serve the majority of the people, or are the majority of the people here to serve the economy and those few who own the largest parts of it?

Until the 1980s, the consensus answer was the former, and the primary regulator of the economy, the government, largely worked to protect working people. Since the "Reagan Revolution," however, the issue has rarely been raised, as media, the courts, and the majority of politicians of both parties have chosen the latter answer.

And the principal vehicle used by those who control most of the economy to regulate it to their favor and against average working people has been monopoly.

Monopoly (using the term in its broadest sense, to include everything from a single company controlling a market to a half dozen companies working in a cartel-like fashion) is why working people's pay hasn't gone up since 1982, when President Ronald Reagan's Federal Trade Commission and Department of Justice stopped enforcing the anti-monopoly laws.[4]

The rich have gotten fabulously richer since then. Consumers, when harmed or ripped off, have largely been stripped of their legal powers to hold businesses accountable. America now lags behind other countries in innovation, which is why (as one small example) we have the highest pharmaceutical and health care costs in the world.

Our streets are filled with guns, our schools have been stripped of books and school supplies, and our food is so deficient in nutrients (vegetables today have about half the nutrients they did in 1950[5]) that we are experiencing a malnutrition-induced obesity epidemic.

Monopoly is why it's so hard to start a new business (particularly a small, local business) and so difficult for existing local and regional companies to survive. It's why pension funds have been "legally" stolen, and the vast majority of workers have lost or been denied the right to representation in the workplace.

Monopoly is why so many of our politicians seem to work in lockstep against the interests of average people and in favor of big business and the very rich. More and more democracies around the world are sliding into autocracy and oligarchy. Our courts have repealed laws passed in the first decade of the 1900s—both federally and in the states—that made it a crime for corporations to contribute "any thing of value" to political campaigns, even though voters overwhelmingly support limits on campaign contributions.

Because of monopolies, billionaires pay lower tax rates than you do, and the nation's largest companies not only usually pay no taxes at all but also get billions every year in subsidies funded with your tax dollars. So many families have fallen out of the middle class that this country is experiencing epidemics of suicide, opioid addiction, and divorce. Our defense budget is bloated, while our returning soldiers find it harder and harder to get jobs or services.

Although it's almost never discussed in our highly monopolized media, monopoly is why right-wing radio and TV are found in every nook and cranny, every town small and large across America, while progressive media is marginalized. It's why our politics are broken and foreign governments have been able to manipulate our elections and seize control of so many of our politicians.

The simple fact is that everything—literally everything—exists in some sort of a balanced relationship with everything else and does so because everything obeys simple rules to maintain that balance. Break the rules—as both business monopolies and cancer do—and the balance collapses.

Most of these rules are the rules of nature; our bodies, for example, have a complex and delicately balanced immune system that detects when a cell has mutated in a way that it's breaking the rules, and the immune system takes that cell apart, recycling its internal materials. But lacking the proper nutrients to maintain its normal functions, our immune systems—the rule-keepers—become less and less able to do their jobs. The result is disease and, in the worst cases, cancer.

Similarly, when the rule-keepers in political and economic systems are compromised, monopolies emerge just like cancer does in bodies. Those monopolies suck all the resources out of the system and eventually either change it so much that it's no longer functional or push it so far that it collapses.

During the first few months of a tumor's growth, if it were self-aware, it'd be quite proud of its ability to reroute blood and nutrients away from other cells and into itself. Similarly, rule-breakers often are quite successful, at least for a while. Consider the organized-crime "mob" and its dominance of the construction and real estate industries in New York up until the past few decades.

For some time, mob- and oligarch-connected real estate developers like Donald Trump were able to build themselves empires based on unfairly winning against competitors who played by the rules and didn't lie about their properties or hook up with overseas criminal billionaires looking to stash ill-gotten gains or hire illegal undocumented laborers from Poland.

In the United States, in large part because of massive changes in the rules of business starting during the Reagan Revolution, we're now in the cancer stage of capitalism. Similarly, our environment is badly out of balance and could be described as cancerous. So far, most of the victims have been those who can't fight back: workers who've seen their pay and rights crash, and people whose homes and lives have been ravaged by out-of-control weather systems they can't control or defend against.

But, like an immune system desperately trying to fight back against a fast-growing tumor, workers are wising up and starting to demand that the rules return to the kind of balance that kept wages high and inequality low before Reagan; similarly, nations around the world are reacting to the climate crisis by cutting their carbon outputs and moving rapidly to renewable energy sources. The question now is whether the cancer of monopoly has gone so far that it's like an end-stage metastasis; will Western democracy survive its assault?

Monopoly doesn't threaten just the business world. It spreads its cancerous tentacles into politics as well, destroying the ability of government to make policy that allows free people to make their own decisions about their own lives.

As President Teddy Roosevelt, the great trust buster, said, "There can be no effective control of corporations while their political activity remains. To put an end to it will be neither a short nor an easy task."[6]

Adam Smith wrote, in *Wealth of Nations*, "[T]he monopoly which our manufacturers have obtained against us. . . . [L]ike an overgrown standing army, they have become formidable to the government, and upon many occasions intimidate the legislature."[7]

If the economic engine of the United States is to be turned back to benefiting the majority of the people rather than today's small minority, breaking up monopolies will be one of the most powerful tools to bring about that change.

Monopoly Kills: Competition, Creativity, and Americans

Left to its own logic, Big Business cares only about profit. With the rules that are currently in place, Big Business is *encouraged* to ruthlessly pursue profit at the expense of workers, communities, and the environment.

Just like in the game of Monopoly, this will eventually result in a situation where one person, or company, owns nearly everything (at least sector by sector). This happened with the railroads at the end of the 19th century, with the electric lines at the beginning of the 20th century, and with copper telephone lines in the mid-20th century in America under the Bell System, aka "Ma Bell."

Each time, it has taken the heavy hand of government to break up these monopolies, because monopolies aren't just bad for consumers, they're also bad for the economy as a whole.

In the extreme case, when one company controls a set of goods or services, that company gets to set its prices at whatever level it wants. Beyond that, with no competition, a monopolist has no incentive to invest in research and development, and no incentive to improve its own infrastructure or to hire more people. This means that the company simply sucks money out of the economy to sit in corporate coffers, or to be paid out as extravagant bonus packages for its board of directors and executives, exacerbating income and wealth inequality.

Worse yet, without any competition, a monopolistic company's main rival becomes the federal government, because the federal government is the only entity with enough power to break up or restrain the monopolistic company.

A monopolistic company will, thus, inevitably try to co-opt the government through lobbying, campaign contributions, or outright bribes. Co-opting the government becomes the only way that the company can retain its monopoly and ensure that the profits keep rolling in, so that the bonuses and dividends can continue to be paid out.

In the real world, this happens even in situations where a true monopoly doesn't exist.

Part 1 of this book shows (1) how the United States was founded in resistance to monopoly; (2) how the Founders discussed the different forms of monopoly, from economic to intellectual; and (3) why some monopolies—*natural monopolies*—are not only good, but essential as a bulwark against the privatization of the commons, and to protect the General Welfare.

Part 2 tells the story of (1) President Franklin Delano Roosevelt warning that fascism would come to America in the form of monopolists and vested capital; (2) how Robert Bork masterminded the dismantling of America's antitrust enforcement; and (3) how deregulation further destroyed Main Street across America and stole Americans' leisure time and work lives.

Part 3 (1) shows some key sectors where monopolies are limiting America's economy and choking America's middle class; (2) shows how monopoly stifles life on this planet beyond the realm of simple economic accounting; and (3) proposes solutions that range from political advocacy that each of us can take on as individuals to big (and necessary) systemic changes to avert economic, social, and climate catastrophe.

As America struggles to recover from the extraordinary economic incompetence of the Trump administration and its callous and erratic response to the coronavirus crisis, pretty much every thread and detail in this book acquires a new urgency and significance.

The lessons of history are clear, though: crises represent opportunities, both for monopolists and for those who would regulate them and return economic power to smaller and more local enterprises. This is as much true today as it was in the 1930s.

As the wheel of history continues to turn, the prescriptions in this book are more urgent than at any other moment in our lifetimes.

PART ONE

America Was Founded on Resistance to Monopoly

Birthed in the Fight Against Monopoly

America was birthed in a fight against monopoly.

There's a pervasive myth in America—promoted by wealthy anti-tax activists—that the Revolutionary War was fought because colonists didn't want to pay taxes to England. While that sentiment was certainly widespread, the spark that lit the fuse of the Revolution was monopoly and a giant tax *cut* for the world's largest corporation, not an increase in taxes.

By 1773, Great Britain had a stranglehold on the economy of the colonies, enforced through the British East India Company, which held monopoly rights to much of the commerce with North America.[1]

The Company, whose stock was heavily held by the British royal family and senior government officials, successfully lobbied Parliament for a variety of restrictions on commercial activity in the colonies, including a ban on the manufacture of most high-end products, such as clothing, and an absolute monopoly on the wholesaling of tea to the colonies.

Up and down the East Coast, small tea shops and tea importers reacted with rage to the Tea Act of 1773, which gave the East India Company a massive tax break, eliminating all tax on their tea sold into the colonies, and expanded their monopoly on the tea business. Small importers, who'd been buying in the London markets or from Dutch trading companies to sell to teahouses from Boston to Washington, DC, found themselves undercut by the tax-free Company tea.

The citizens of Boston and surrounding areas covered their faces, massed in the streets, and destroyed the property of a giant global corporation. Declaring an end to global trade run by the East India Company that was destroying local economies, this small minority started a revolution with an act of rebellion later called the Boston Tea Party.

In a rare-book store around 2000, I came upon a first edition of *A Retrospect of the Boston Tea-Party, With a Memoir of George R. T. Hewes, a Survivor of the Little Band of Patriots Who Drowned the Tea in Boston Harbour in 1773*. Because the identities of the Boston Tea Party participants had been hidden (other than Samuel Adams), and all were sworn to secrecy for the next 50 years, this is the only existing first-person account of the event by a participant.

Hewes's description suggests that the Boston Tea Party resembled today's growing protests against corporate monopolies, as well as the efforts of small towns to protect themselves from chain-store retailers, frackers, toxic waste sites, coal-fired power plants, and factory farms.

Although schoolchildren are usually taught that the American Revolution was a rebellion against "taxation without representation," akin to modern-day conservative taxpayer revolts, in fact what led to the Revolution was rage against a transnational corporation that, by the 1760s, dominated trade from China to India to the Caribbean and controlled nearly all commerce to and from North America, with subsidies and special dispensation from the British crown.

Hewes wrote, "The [East India] Company received permission to transport tea, free of all duty, from Great Britain to America," allowing it to wipe out New England–based tea wholesalers and mom-and-pop stores and take over the tea business in all of America.

Hence, it was no longer the small vessels of private merchants, who went to vend tea for their own account in the ports of the colonies, but, on the contrary, ships of an enormous burthen, that transported immense quantities of this commodity. . . . The colonies were now arrived at the decisive moment when they must cast the dye, and determine their course.[2]

Hewes, dressed as an Indian, disguised his face with coal dust and joined crowds of other men in silently hacking apart the chests of tea and throwing them into the harbor. In all, the 342 chests of tea—over 90,000 pounds—thrown overboard that night were enough to make 24 million cups of tea and were valued by the East India Company at 9,659 pounds sterling, or, in today's currency, just over $1 million.

In response, the British Parliament immediately passed the Boston Port Act, stating that the port of Boston would be closed until the citizens of Boston reimbursed the East India Company for the tea they had destroyed. The colonists refused.

A year and a half later, the colonists again defied the East India Company and Great Britain by taking on British troops in an armed conflict at Lexington and Concord (the "shots heard 'round the world") on April 19, 1775.

That war—triggered by a transnational corporation and its government patrons trying to deny American colonists a fair and competitive local marketplace—ended with independence for the colonies.

The revolutionaries had put the East India Company in its place with the Boston Tea Party, and that, they thought, was the end of that.

Unfortunately, the Boston Tea Party was not the end; 150 years later, during the so-called Gilded Age, powerful rail, steel, and oil interests rose up to begin a new form of political system to benefit the wealthy and their corporations. America's economic royalists captured the newly formed Republican Party in the 1880s and have been working to establish a permanent wealthy and ruling class in this country ever since.

The Founders Challenge Monopoly

The more things change, the old saying goes, the more they stay the same. It's true, at least with regard to giant corporate interests fighting regulation and seizing control of governments that might try to restrain them.

The year of 1776 had a huge impact on the future of the world. Not only did Thomas Jefferson and friends declare that they'd no longer submit to the military, commercial, and political power of Great Britain, but one of the world's great analysts of capitalism, Adam Smith, published his book *An Inquiry into the Nature and Causes of the Wealth of Nations*.[3]

At the same time that the American colonists were decrying the monopoly that the East India Company held over them, Smith was criticizing the Company—and the others who had succeeded in creating monopoly—in Great Britain.

He started out by calling for a return to "natural liberty"—competition—to return to Great Britain's economy "especially if the privileges of corporations . . . were abolished." In order to make the economy work correctly, Smith said, Great Britain must "break down the exclusive privileges of corporations" and take from them the power to regulate employment "so that a poor workman, when thrown out of employment either in one trade or in one place, may seek for it in another trade or in another place, without the fear either of a prosecution or of a removal."

He condemned the actions of the big corporations that then dominated Britain's economy, noting that even military officers wouldn't be as greedy to maintain their numbers and positions, and oppose any laws that might regulate their behavior, as were the monopolistic corporations:

Were the officers of the army to oppose with the same zeal and unanimity any reduction in the number of forces, with which master manufacturers set themselves against every law that is likely to increase the number of their rivals in the home market; . . . to attack with violence and outrage the proposers of any such regulation; to attempt to reduce the army would be as dangerous as it has now become to attempt to diminish in any respect the monopoly which our manufacturers have obtained against us.

Referencing the East India Company, Smith wrote, "This monopoly has so much increased the number of some particular tribes of them, that, like an overgrown standing army, they have become formidable to the government, and upon many occasions intimidate the legislature." Indeed, many members of the Great Britain legislature at that time either were afraid of the Company and its colleagues or owned so much stock in them that their votes aligned with the monopolists' interests—a situation not unlike what we see today in our legislatures.

"The member of parliament who supports every pro-posal for strengthening this monopoly," Smith wrote, "is sure to acquire . . . great popularity and influence with an order of men whose numbers and wealth render them of great importance."

On the other hand, the Company and others routinely punished—severely—those legislators who dared call for its regulation, regardless of how much power or reputation those legislators may have had. Nothing, literally nothing, Smith said, could restrain these corporations, and everybody knew it.

If he [a legislator] opposes them, on the contrary, and still more if he has authority enough to be able to thwart them, neither the most acknowledged probity, nor the highest rank, nor the greatest public services, can protect him from the most infamous abuse and detraction, from personal insults, nor sometimes from real danger, arising from the insolent outrage of furious and disappointed monopolists.

Smith went on to recommend that the British Parliament take on the monopolists while preventing more from arising. "The legislature," he said, directed "by an extensive view of the general good," should "be particularly careful neither to establish any new monopolies of this kind, nor to extend further those which are already established."

On the other side of the ocean, Jefferson and his compatriots eagerly read Smith, that day's revolutionary economic thinker, along the lines of Thomas Piketty today. Jefferson so absorbed Smith's lessons about the dangers of monopoly that he argued—and nearly took down the Constitution itself in fighting for it—that the Bill of Rights should contain an explicit ban on monopoly.

When he was the US envoy to Paris in 1786, he repeatedly attacked specific monopolistic industries. The tobacco monopolies that had been granted by Great Britain and France were particular recipients of his bile. In a January 24, 1786, letter to the governor of Virginia, he wrote,

> *I have been fully sensible of the baneful influence on the commerce of France and America, which this double [tobacco] monopoly will have. I have struck at its root here, and spared no pains to have the form itself demolished, but it has been in vain. The persons interested in it are too powerful to be opposed, even by the interest of the whole country.*[4]

Jefferson wasn't immune to fear of retribution from large monopolistic enterprises. The next sentence in his letter says, "I mention this matter in confidence, as a knowledge of it might injure any further endeavors to attain the same object."

On May 8 of that year, he wrote to James Ross, revisiting the topic. "My hopes, therefore, are weak, though not quite desperate. When they become so, it will remain to look about for the best palliative this monopoly can bear."[5]

In another letter on the same day, this one to T. Pleasants, Jefferson wrote, "I was moreover engaged in endeavors to have the monopoly, in the purchase of this article, in this country, suppressed. My hopes on that subject are not desperate, but neither are they flattering."[6]

He revisited the topic in a half dozen or more letters that year.

But it was the "operating system," or constitution, that would direct the future of America—including the economic future—that most concerned Jefferson. When James Madison sent him a first draft of the new US Constitution that they'd worked out that summer and fall in Philadelphia, Jefferson's response was blunt.

On December 20, 1787, he replied to his protégé:

I will now tell you what I do not like. First, the omission of a bill of rights, providing clearly, and without the aid of sophism, for freedom of religion, freedom of the press, protection against standing armies, restriction of monopolies, the eternal and unremitting force of the habeas corpus laws, and trials by jury in all matters of fact triable by the laws of the land, and not by the laws of nations.[7]

Every item except the restriction of monopolies made its way into the Bill of Rights.

But Jefferson couldn't let it go; he'd been thinking about this for years, and he had written about it in some of his private papers such as his diary, and spoken about it in conversations with close friends. A constitution, after all, would become the supreme law of the land for generations to come.

Although the Constitution had come into effect on March 4, 1789, six months later he was still writing about the matter to Madison. On September 6, 1789, he opened his letter by saying that he was compelled to reach out to Madison "because a subject comes into my head."

At its core, Jefferson said, was "[t]he question, whether one generation of men has a right to bind another" because "it is a question of . . . the fundamental principles of every government."[8]

Among those principles was the need to prevent monopolists from rising up and taking over America, locking us into a rigid class system that kept small economic players out of the marketplace while encumbering working-class families with multigenerational debt (like student loan debt is, by law, today, thanks to George W. Bush's 2005 bankruptcy "reform").

Noting how quickly wealth and business interests can corrupt government, Jefferson wrote, "Various checks are opposed to every legislative proposition. Factions get possession of the public councils, bribery corrupts them, personal interests lead them astray from the general interests of their constituents."

The solution? Among other things, Jefferson said that the Constitution should address "monopolies in commerce."[9]

Like Adam Smith, he never lived to see the day.

Madison's Vision:
Government to Fight Factions

Government is the agency that we collectively create (at least we do in a democratic republic) to manage the natural monopolies that we all use, share, and/or need: the atmosphere, water and waterways, septic and waste, public roads and skyways, police and fire, and, most broadly, the entire infrastructure of commerce and the public good.

The whole idea of government grew out of ancient families, tribes, and clans, who worked together to protect the youngest, eldest, and weakest members of then-hunter-gatherer communities.

Particularly since the agricultural revolution, what we call government has often been twisted and manipulated by the very wealthy (kings/empires/fascism/feudalism/etc.), but its core functions when it works best are still found in the Preamble to the US Constitution: to provide for justice, defense, tranquility, liberty, and the general welfare of the people.

If any one faction—to use Madison's word from *Federalist*, no. 10, to describe people who would put their own interest above those of their fellow citizens—were to rise up and dominate a government, the republic would inevitably be weakened. Madison wrote, "By a faction, I understand a number of citizens . . . who are united and actuated by some common impulse of passion, or of interest, *adversed* [opposed] to the rights of other citizens, or to the permanent and aggregate interests of the community [emphasis mine]."[10]

Madison's idea was that the core function of government was to *fight* factions, as he laid out in both *Federalist*, no. 10, and many of his commentaries on the Constitution. In this regard, there was virtual unanimity among the Founders and the Framers of the Constitution. They'd fought a war of independence against a government that was in cahoots with the world's largest corporation and had no intention of letting such a monopoly happen again on these shores, as documented earlier. Only government, they knew, had the power—essentially, the police power and rulemaking power—to defy the economic elite.

The monopolists know this truth as well. If government were directly responsible and responsive to The People, it wouldn't dance exclusively to the tune of the very largest corporations. But if the monopolists could convince The People that the government was their enemy, then they would be able to wrest control away from The People. More on that in the chapter "How the Monopolists Stole the US Government."

The Founders on Patents and Copyrights

There are two basic types of monopoly: those created by a business growing so large that it controls a marketplace, and those explicitly created by government. At the time of the writing of the Constitution, the term *monopoly* was generally used to describe either corporate monopolies like the British East India Company or government-created ones like patents and copyrights.

Much of this book is devoted to the East India Company types of monopoly, but the monopolies created by patent and copyright laws are important as well, particularly because these systems can either foster or stifle innovation and markets.

The US Constitution, in Article 1, Section 8, explicitly authorizes Congress to pass laws, "[t]o promote the Progress of Science and useful Arts, by securing for limited Times to Authors and Inventors the exclusive Right to their respective Writings and Discoveries."

In both cases, these government-granted monopolies were intended to "promote the progress of science and useful arts" by two mechanisms. The first incentivizes authors and inventors to produce useful works by giving them a financial reason, since their monopoly patent or copyright can be assigned or sold to others. The second, particularly with regard to patents, is to encourage inventors to publish (via the Patent Office) and share with the world the details of their inventions *so they can be expanded on or inspire other inventions.*

As Sir Isaac Newton wrote to his then-friend Robert Hooke in 1675, "If I have seen further, it is by standing on the shoulders of Giants."[11] Inventions don't just spring wholly formed from the forehead of inventors the way Athena did from Zeus in Greek mythology; they're almost always built on something preceding them.

And encouraging inventors to publish their inventions in detail—as the patent process requires—means that other inventors can metaphorically stand on the shoulders of their predecessors. The same is true of ideas presented in copyrighted books, songs, movies, and so on.

Although ancient Greece and Venice in the 1400s tried patent monopolies, at the time of the founding of our republic these were still considered novel ideas. As Thomas Jefferson noted in a letter to Isaac McPherson, "[I]t is a fact, as far as I am informed, that England was, until we copied her, the only country on earth which ever, by a general law, gave a legal right to the exclusive use of an idea."[12]

Nonetheless, following the Patent Act of 1790, Jefferson marveled at the result. He wrote to Benjamin Vaughn,

An act of Congress authorizing the issuing of patents for new discoveries has given a spring to invention beyond my conception. Being an instrument in granting the patents [Jefferson worked on the panel that approved patents for a

short time], I am acquainted with their discoveries. Many of them indeed are trifling, but there are some of great consequence, which have been proved by practice, and others which, if they stand the same proof, will produce great effect.[13]

The following year, 1791, France followed the United States and created a patent law, and over the following decades the practice spread across Europe and, eventually, the entire industrialized world.

In the United States there are two kinds of patents, "design" and "utility." Design patents, valid for 14 or 15 years, are basically protection for how things *look*, be they an iPhone or an ornamental filigree pattern. The far more common utility patents protect the actual function of a device: technically, they protect compositions, processes, and machines, and they last for 20 years from the filing date.

Patents and their terms have been relatively short since the founding of America and have thus encouraged innovation and invention; the same can't be said for copyrights, which have a pretty amazing history, largely influenced, apparently, by Mickey Mouse.

The Copyright Act of 1790 set copyrights for writing and art at 14 years, with a 14-year renewal if the author or creator was still alive. In 1831, the initial period was doubled to 28 years, with a 14-year renewal if the author was still alive. The renewal period was equalized to the initial copyright in 1909—28 years initially with a 28-year renewal for living authors or creators.

A few years later, in 1928, Walt Disney created a cartoon character, Mickey Mouse, and his copyright under the law at the time could have lasted 56 years—the initial 28 plus the renewal—until 1984.

Eight years before Mickey would have expired, Congress acted, making the initial term of copyrights the lifetime of the creator or author (Walt was still alive) plus an additional 50 years after his or her death, and granting to corporations like Disney retroactive application of the new term with a 75-year renewal term. This pushed Mickey's expiration out to 2003.

But the mouse maintained his popularity, and Disney wanted to prevent anybody else from getting in on the act. Thus, in 1998, one of Los Angeles's congressmen decided to help Disney with the Sonny Bono Copyright Term Extension Act, extending the copyright on works owned by an individual to the life of the author plus 70 years, and corporate-owned works to 95 years from the first time published or 120 years from the time the work was created (but not published), whichever came first.

Thus, Mickey now expires in 2023, so any day now there will probably be another update to the law.[14]

Jefferson shared some thoughts on the topic of government-granted monopolies such as patents and copyrights in his previously mentioned letter to Isaac McPherson:

> *He who receives an idea from me, receives instruction himself without lessening mine; as he who lights his taper [candle] at mine, receives light without darkening me. That ideas should freely spread from one to another over the globe, for the moral and mutual instruction of man, and improvement of his condition, seems to have been peculiarly and benevolently designed by nature, when she made them, like fire, expansible over all space, without lessening their*

density in any point, and like the air in which we breathe,
move, and have our physical being, incapable of confine-
ment or exclusive appropriation. Inventions then cannot, in
nature, be a subject of property.

There's no record of any of the Founders, however, ever
weighing in on cartoon mice.

The Monopolists Rise Up

When, in the 1880s, the state of Ohio began threatening
Standard Oil Trust of Ohio with the corporate death penalty,
breaking up and dissolving the corporation and selling off its
assets, John D. Rockefeller and his monopolist buddies publicly called for states to change their corporate governance
laws to get around all of the restrictions that Ohio and most
other states had placed on them.

New Jersey heard the call and thus became the first state to
engage in what was then called "charter-mongering"—changing its corporate charter rules to satisfy the desires of the
nation's largest businesses. In 1875, its legislature abolished
maximum capitalization (size) limits.

In 1888, the New Jersey Legislature took another huge
and dramatic step to help out Rockefeller by authorizing—
for the first time in the history of the United States—New
Jersey–chartered companies to hold stock in other companies. The Standard Oil Trust was legally still in business (Ohio
outlawed trusts in 1892, but by then Rockefeller had moved
his company to New Jersey), renamed Standard Oil of New
Jersey. (It's now BP.)

As New Jersey and then Delaware threw out old restrictions on corporate behavior, allowing corporations to have interlocking boards, to live forever, to define themselves for "any legal purpose," to own stock in other corporations, and so on, corporations began to move both their corporate charters and, in some cases, their headquarters to the charter-mongering states.

By 1900, trusts for everything from ribbons to bread to cement to alcohol had moved to Delaware or New Jersey, leaving 26 corporate trusts controlling, from those states, more than 80% of production in their markets.

There was pushback in New York, though. In 1894, the Central Labor Union of New York City campaigned for the New York State Supreme Court to revoke the charter of Standard Oil Trust of New York for "a pattern of abuses," and the court agreed and dissolved the company.

By 1912, New Jersey Governor Woodrow Wilson was alarmed by the behavior of corporations in his state and "pressed through changes [that took effect in 1913] intended to make New Jersey's corporations less favorable to concentrated financial power."[15]

But as New Jersey began to pull back from charter-mongering, Delaware stepped into the fray, passing in 1915 laws similar to but even easier on corporations than New Jersey's. Delaware, over the next few decades, continued to strip away its corporate accountability rules so that today, Harvard Business Services notes on its website devoted to incorporating in Delaware that more than two-thirds of all corporations listed in the Fortune 500 are Delaware corporations, including fully 80% of all companies that did public offerings in 2017. Just the year 2016 saw more than 200,000 new companies starting as Delaware corporations or LLCs, bringing the state's total up to over 1.3 million.[16]

Progressives Fight Back

In reaction to public disgust over the predatory and monopolistic behavior of these corporate giants, the "Progressive Era" of Teddy Roosevelt's presidency (1901–1909) saw numerous laws passed that were designed to restrain bad corporate behavior. The most well-known was the Tillman Act of 1907, which made it a felony for corporations to give money to federal politicians' campaigns.

The Tillman Act was based, in part, on numerous state laws, like this one that Wisconsin passed in 1905 (and was taken off the books in 1954):

> Political contributions by corporations. *No corporation doing business in this state shall pay or contribute, or offer consent or agree to pay or contribute, directly or indirectly, any money, property, free service of its officers or employees or thing of value to any political party, organization, committee or individual for any political purpose whatsoever, or for the purpose of influencing legislation of any kind, or to promote or defeat the candidacy of any person for nomination, appointment or election to any political office.*[17]

The penalty for an individual (even a lawyer or lobbyist representing a corporation) breaking this law on behalf of a corporation was not just a large fine but a two-year prison term, and if the corporation itself was found to have violated the law, it faced the corporate death penalty: "*dissolution* of the corporation and sale of its assets."

But 1921 saw the end of all that, when Republican Warren G. Harding successfully ran for president on a platform of tax cuts, deregulation, and privatization. His twin slogans were "More business in government [privatize], less government in business [deregulate]" and "Return to normalcy [take taxes back down to where they were before World War I]."

When elected, he lowered the top tax rate from 91% to 25%, producing a huge sugar high for the economy. It kicked off the Roaring Twenties and led straight to the Great Crash of 1929, which was made much worse by Harding's successful deregulation of the banks and brokerage houses.

During the Republican Great Depression of the 1930s, the American business landscape was littered with failed and failing small- and medium-sized companies. They were easy pickings for those larger enterprises that were still cash rich and could buy the struggling companies out of near-bankruptcy. Another strategy many monopolists employed was to simply compete directly with the struggling companies and run them out of business.

Since the Trump Crash of 2020, we've seen a similar dynamic at work. Giant corporations got massive bailouts and trillions in loans from the Fed, while small enterprises have struggled and failed by the millions. The result is a substantial further consolidation of American monopoly that will impact our business landscape for a generation.

Between the 1920s and the 1980s, all US states amended their constitutions or changed their laws to make it easier for large corporations to do business without having to answer to the citizens of the state, without size limits, and with infinite life spans.

Part 2 of this book shows how, during that same period, corporate America accumulated massive amounts of wealth and turned that wealth toward legal and political power that has destroyed America's middle class and wiped out Main Street businesses across the country.

PART TWO

Conservatives
and Modern Monopolies
vs. the Middle Class

Monopoly in the 20th Century: Roosevelt Warns of Concentrated Wealth and Fascism

On April 20, 1938, the Associated Church Press—a group of reporters for religious magazines and newspapers—met with President Franklin D. Roosevelt in Washington, DC. One of their first questions was, "I would like to ask you, how great is the danger of fascism in this country? We hear about fascism-baiting in the United States."

FDR's answer was blunt, and it reveals a lot to us today of how Americans thought of "fascist" enterprises back in that day.

"I think there is danger," he replied to the question, "because every time you have the breaking down or failure of some process we have been accustomed to for a long time, the tendency is for that process, because of the breakdown, to get into the hands of a very small group."

He then spoke directly to the issue of centralized—and distant—ownership or control of business by powerful interests, in this case the banks in New York. FDR contracted adult polio at age 39 and was partially paralyzed from it, so he spent a lot of time in Warm Springs, Georgia, where people stricken by polio could float and lightly exercise in the warm, mineral-rich water. On several of his visits, he'd heard from the people who lived in Georgia that they weren't happy with the way the "local" utility was refusing to extend electric power out to rural areas like the ones around Warm Springs.

"One of our southern states that I spend a lot of time in," he said, giving an example to illustrate his point, "has a very large power company, the Georgia Power Company.

There are a lot of people in Georgia that want to own and run Georgia power, but it is owned by Commonwealth and Southern in New York City.... Georgia has plenty of money with which to extend electric light lines to the rural communities, and the officers of Georgia Power Company themselves want it Georgia-owned or Georgia-run. But they have to go to New York for the money. If it were not for that, we would not have any utility problem, and all of them would be owned in the districts which they serve, and they would get rid of this financial control."[1]

But it wasn't just that rural Georgia was being screwed by profit taking in New York and was powerless in the face of it. The controlling of electricity in Georgia by this for-profit privately owned monopoly meant that rural Americans in that state would still have to light their homes with kerosene and couldn't even turn on a radio.

It also meant that workers were often stripped of appropriate compensation for their work. "You take the new lumber companies that want to start on this wonderful process of making print paper out of yellow pine," FDR continued. "One reason for the low wages of the workers in the pulp mills of Mississippi, Georgia, North Carolina, and South Carolina is that practically all profits go north; they do not stay south. If the profits stayed south, the whole scale of living would go up."

And then he brought it all back to the word *fascism*, which the dictionaries of the day defined as the merger of state and corporate power, a process that was well underway in Italy—where Mussolini had dissolved the elected parliament and replaced it with the Chamber of the Fascist Corporations, where the Italian equivalent of each congressional district was represented by its largest industry instead of an elected member—and Hitler and Tojo had both moved to bring powerful business leaders and industrial tycoons into government.

"I am greatly in favor of decentralization," FDR wrapped up his answer to that question, "and yet the tendency is, every time we have trouble in private industry, to concentrate it all the more in New York. Now that is, ultimately, fascism."

Nine days later, President Roosevelt brought up the issue again in his April 29, 1938, "Message to Congress on the Concentration of Economic Power."[2]

> *Unhappy events abroad have re-taught us two simple truths about the liberty of a democratic people.*
>
> *The first truth is that the liberty of a democracy is not safe if the people tolerate the growth of private power to a point where it becomes stronger than their democratic state itself. That, in its essence, is fascism—ownership of government by an individual, by a group, or by any other controlling private power.*
>
> *The second truth is that the liberty of a democracy is not safe if its business system does not provide employment and produce and distribute goods in such a way as to sustain an acceptable standard of living.*

Speaking of the captains of industry who, in the election two years earlier he had said, "hate me, and I welcome their hatred," FDR laid out the state of things that three previous Republican administrations (Harding, Coolidge, Hoover) and their deregulatory fervor had brought about:

> *Among us today a concentration of private power without equal in history is growing.*

This concentration is seriously impairing the economic effectiveness of private enterprise as a way of providing employment for labor and capital and as a way of assuring a more equitable distribution of income and earnings among the people of the nation as a whole.

Shifting from the rhetorical to the concrete, he gave a few startling examples:

Statistics of the Bureau of Internal Revenue reveal the following amazing figures for 1935:

Ownership of corporate assets: Of all corporations reporting from every part of the nation, one-tenth of 1 percent of them owned 52 percent of the assets of all of them.

And to clinch the point: Of all corporations reporting, less than 5 percent of them owned 87 percent of all assets of all of them.

Income and profits of corporations: Of all the corporations reporting from every part of the country, one-tenth of 1 percent of them earned 50 percent of the net income of all of them.

And to clinch the point: Of all the manufacturing corporations reporting, less than 4 percent of them earned 84 percent of all the net profits of all of them.

FDR pointed out that the Republican Great Depression (what it was called until the early 1950s[3]) had played a role in this process by weakening small businesses and often forcing them to sell out to larger interests or to mortgage themselves to big players, generally in distant cities.

The Republican policies he was noting produced vast wealth for a small number of monopolists and stripped workers of their wages and security. And the monopolists were, throughout the Roaring Twenties, using the Harding/Coolidge/Hoover deregulation of the marketplace to concentrate ownership of America's productive enterprises in their own tiny hands. The peak of the trend had been in the summer of 1929, when the market was at its top.

"[I]n that year," FDR told Congress, "three-tenths of 1 percent of our population received 78 percent of the dividends reported by individuals. This has roughly the same effect as if, out of every 300 persons in our population, one person received 78 cents out of every dollar of corporate dividends, while the other 299 persons divided up the other 22 cents between them."

But it wasn't just wealth in the form of stock and business ownership that was concentrating. As the circle of ownership of entire industries was becoming smaller and smaller, that increasingly powerful group of men (and they *were* all men) were able to redefine the workplace so they could take more and more out of the paychecks of their workers and keep it for themselves.

By 1936, FDR said, "[f]orty-seven percent of all American families and single individuals living alone had incomes of less than $1,000 for the year; and at the other end of the ladder a little less than 1 percent of the nation's families received incomes which in dollars and cents reached the same total as the incomes of the 47 percent at the bottom."

Ask "average men and women in every part of the country," FDR said, what this concentration of wealth and its attendant political power meant. "Their answer," he told Congress, "is that if there is that danger, it comes from that concentrated private economic power which is struggling so hard to master our democratic government."

They were doing it through monopoly. FDR said that "interlocking spheres of influence over channels of investment and through the use of financial devices like holding companies and strategic minority interests" meant that "[t]he small businessman is unfortunately being driven into a less and less independent position in American life."

Big business, the president said, while "masking itself as a system of free enterprise after the American model . . . is in fact becoming a concealed cartel system after the European model."

He wrapped up the speech with a specific call to take on monopoly in America. It was a call that echoed through the next three decades. "Once it is realized that business monopoly in America paralyzes the system of free enterprise on which it is grafted," FDR said, "and is as fatal to those who manipulate it as to the people who suffer beneath its impositions, action by the government to eliminate these artificial restraints will be welcomed by industry throughout the nation."

Monopoly and Fascism in America Today

Today, things are even worse than in FDR's time.

"The top 1 percent of families captured 58 percent of total real income growth per family from 2009 to 2014," wrote economist Emmanuel Saez for the Washington Center for Equitable Growth.[4]

In large part, the concentration of both wealth and income has come about in the era since the Reagan presidency and the introduction of "Reaganomics." In the 40 years prior to Reagan, income and wealth among working people was growing at a *faster rate* than it was for the top 1%. Since Reaganomics was instituted—a system within which we're still operating—the wealth and income of the top 1% has exploded.

When Reagan came into office in 1981 and welcomed the monopolists back into government, everything shifted. Where we once had wide and celebrated local and regional diversity in beer brewing, for example (remember "Milwaukee's Finest" and when Coors had to be smuggled out of Colorado?), today we have instead two corporations that produce over 90% of all the beer consumed in the United States, and one of the two, Anheuser-Busch, is now largely owned by Belgian and Brazilian investors.[5]

If you want to relax with the internet instead of a beer, that marketplace is also highly concentrated.

While South Koreans get internet speeds *200* times faster than what most Americans get, and pay only $27 a month for their service, Susan P. Crawford, author of *Captive Audience: The Telecom Industry and Monopoly Power in the New Gilded Age* and former board member of ICANN, told me that the average American consumer pays around $90 a month for a cell phone with a data plan, compared with the European average of just $19 (and the coverage is better and the data is both faster and unlimited).

Why? Because the European Union doesn't tolerate monopolies as the United States does. There are hundreds of small and feisty competitors across the continent.

On Wall Street, the 20 biggest banks own assets equivalent to 84% of the nation's entire gross domestic product (GDP). And just 12 of those banks own 70% of all the banking assets. That means our entire banking system relies on just a few whales that must be saved at all costs from going belly up, or else the entire system goes belly up.

And consider our food industry. According to Tom Philpott at *Mother Jones* magazine, agriculture oligopolies exist from farm to shelf. Just four companies control 90% of the grain trade. Just three companies control 70% of the American beef industry. And just four companies control 58% of the US pork and chicken producing and processing industries.

On the retail side, Walmart controls a quarter of the entire US grocery market. And just four companies produce 75% of our breakfast cereal, 75% of our snack foods, 60% of our cookies, and half of all the ice cream sold in supermarkets around the nation (Figure 1).

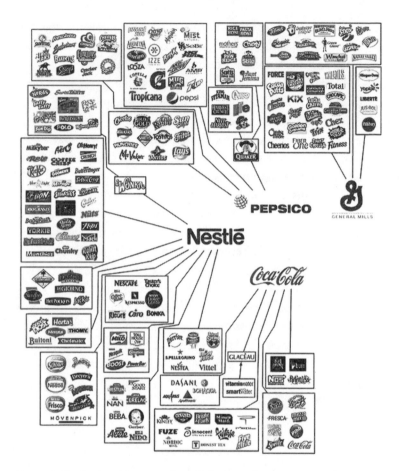

Figure 1. The food and beverage brands that own the grocery store.[6]

Source: Joki Gauthier for Oxfam 2012 (https://www.oxfamamerica.org/explore/research-publications/behind-the-brands/). Reproduced with the permission of Oxfam, Oxfam House, John Smith Drive, Cowley, Oxford OX4 2JY, UK (www.oxfam.org.uk). Oxfam does not necessarily endorse any text or activities that accompany the materials.

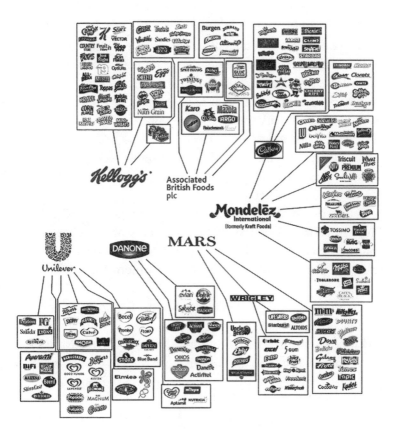

Then there's the health insurance market. Just four health insurance companies—UnitedHealth Group, WellPoint, Aetna, and Humana—control three-quarters of the entire health insurance market. And, as a 2007 study by the group Health Care for America Now uncovered, in 38 states, just two insurers controlled 57% of the market. In 15 states, one insurer controlled 60% of the market.

Since there's no functional competition in such a market, prices continue to go higher and higher while the profits for these whales skyrocket too.

In the cellular phone market, just four companies—AT&T Mobile, Verizon Wireless, T-Mobile, and Sprint Nextel—control 89% of the market. And in the internet arena, just a single corporation—Comcast—controls more than half of the market.

As Adam Smith pointed out, and the Founders of this republic well knew, capitalism is a game that can work for the average person and the small business, but *only* when the rules of the game are set that way. Re-rig those rules to give disproportionate power to the very wealthy, and we slide into what Franklin Roosevelt called fascism.

Since money often equals political power, and political power can be used to rewrite the rules of business and tax law to further concentrate and enhance wealth and income for those paying the lobbyists and members of Congress, this situation not only represents the economic threat of making the marketplace more fragile and liable to crashes like what happened in 1929 but also represents a threat to democracy itself.

Most Americans would be highly offended if the NFL rules were changed to allow whichever team had the most money to have an extra three players on the field at all times. But that's exactly what Reaganomics and its deregulation have brought us in our marketplaces; it's the staggering difficulty that every small business in America faces today.

To understand how to fix this situation so that America's small businesses and middle class can once again thrive, it's important to understand the factors at play that created the vibrant, localized American economy that was the hallmark of mid-20th-century America.

Where Did America's Middle Class Come From?

We hear a lot about "the good old days," as if to suggest that America was always an economically strong nation with a vibrant middle class. But the fact is that we got really, really rich—we being the bottom 90% of Americans—in just a few decades after World War II, as a result of Franklin Roosevelt putting into place the economic theories of Adam Smith and John Maynard Keynes, and those policies holding steady until the election of Ronald Reagan.

In 1900, the average yearly household income was $449[7]— the equivalent of around $13,800 in today's dollars.[8] That kind of income today guarantees a life of want and poverty, and it did in 1900 as well. The only buffer then was the family farm; while today only 1% of Americans live and work on farms, in 1900 it was around 40%.[9]

My wife's grandmother, who was born in 1905, lived on a small (100 acres) farm in central Michigan throughout the Republican Great Depression and for a few decades afterward. I remember Grandma telling us stories about how she bought two dresses and a big bag of salt and a big bag of sugar once a year from the Sears catalog; otherwise, everything they needed was locally sourced or grown. They were "poor," but they weren't experiencing what today we'd call poverty.

So although there were plenty of multimillionaires in 1900—and, in today's dollars, a large handful of billionaires as well—about 40% of America was buffered from the ravages of deep poverty by their farms and their neighbors, while half of America was struggling to live in cities and hanging on to the economic and social edge, barely able to make it year to year.

From 1800 until Reagan—except for the hiccup of the Roaring Twenties and its Republican Great Depression— wages pretty much tracked productivity. The core concept of business was that if a workforce can produce more goods in the same time without sacrificing quality, they should share in the increased profits from the increased sales, if for no other reason than Henry Ford's—so that they'll stick around and work, and the company doesn't have to incur the costs of hiring and retraining associated with employee turnover.

In 1913, most auto manufacturers were paying their employees around $2.25 a day, the equivalent of around $14,000 a year in today's dollars, just slightly below our 2019 federal minimum wage of $7.25. In 1914, Henry Ford famously more than doubled his workers' pay to $5 a day, or $31,000 a year[10] in today's dollars, in part because of the dramatic increase in per-worker productivity he was getting—and wanted to keep—from his assembly line and in part to keep these now highly productive workers on the job; his main incentive was to reduce employee turnover.[11]

World War I and the Republican Great Depression introduced serious noise into the employment and wage statistics until FDR came along and righted the ship of state, but with increasing productivity came increasing wages. By 1950, the yearly average worker income in the United States was clipping along at around $3,000[12] (household income was $3,300, but most households had a single wage earner),[13] or $31,465 per year in today's dollars.[14]

As people returning from World War II were finishing trade school and college and entering the workforce, and the stimulative effect of the GI Bill was raising demand for goods and services, that number had grown to $5,700 a year in 1960, or $48,600 a year per household (there were still few multiple-worker households) in 2019 dollars.

Productivity continued to increase, as did wages, hitting a peak in 1970 of $9,430 per year,[15] or $61,400 in today's dollars. Employers were making more and more money and, trying to avoid paying the top marginal tax rate of 91% (up until 1967 and 73% thereafter), they were plowing that money back into their companies and their employees.

Workers had good union jobs, good benefits in addition to that substantial paycheck, home and car ownership, and annual vacations; they could send their kids to college and even own a small summer home. These were all parts of being "middle class" in America.

Where Did America's Middle Class Go?

Then came the twin hits of trade liberalization in the 1970s—cutting tariffs and allowing cheap imports, so that American workers were competing with lower-paid, then-mostly Japanese workers—and Reagan's massive tax cuts of the 1980s, which explicitly encouraged employers and CEOs to drain as much money out of their companies as they could rather than reinvest it or pay their employees well.

Since the 1970s, productivity has increased by 146%,[16] but wages have actually either stagnated (if looking at household incomes; today many more are two-wage-earner households) or fallen (looking at individual incomes). CEO compensation has rocketed from 30 times the average worker's to hundreds of times, in some industries even thousands of times (for example, Coca-Cola's CEO, James Quincey, gets paid $16.7 million per year—or 1,016 times the typical employee's pay).[17]

The Census Bureau reports that 2016 average *household* income was $57,600[18]—the combined income of (generally) at least two workers, or one worker working more than a single full-time job—a significant fall from its 1970 peak of $61,400 (in today's dollars) for an individual worker with a single full-time job.

Because of Reaganomics, today it takes two or more people working in a household to maintain the standard of living that one worker could sustain prior to the 1980s.

From 1950 to 1970, both wages and productivity pretty much *doubled*, an increase of around 100% (it was in the high 90s, but let's round off to keep things simple).[19]

Using 1950 as a benchmark, between 1970 and 2019 wages went up from around 97% to 114%, but productivity went from 98% above the 1950 number to 243%.[20]

That 130% increase in productivity while holding wages steady led to a massive increase in corporate profits. According to the Federal Reserve Bank of St. Louis (which compiles these statistics), the total profit of all American corporations in 1950 was $33 billion, or about $346 billion in today's dollars. In 1960, it was $55 billion, or $469 billion today. The year 1970 saw total corporate profits at $86 billion, or $560 billion in today's money.[21]

The '70s and '80s were the years of great change, with the end of Bretton Woods (the 1944 international conference that established the modern system of monetary management, including rules for commercial and financial relations among the United States, Canada, Western European countries, Australia, and Japan) and many tariffs in the 1970s, and Reagan's massive tax cuts (and anti-union crusades) in the 1980s.

By 1990, corporate *quarterly* (multiply by 4 for annual) profits were at $413 billion, or $798 billion in today's dollars. In 2000, they hit $770 billion quarterly, or $1.13 trillion a quarter today.

A decade later, in 2010, they were at $1,890 billion (and this after the Great Recession of 2008–2009) every quarter, or $2.19 trillion in today's dollars.

In 2018, the last year the Fed reported as of this writing, corporate profits were at $2.223 trillion—nearly $9 trillion a year or almost half of the entire nation's GDP.[22]

Profits are a pretty reasonable indicator of things, as they're more independent of overall economic activity than most metrics like GDP. From 1970 to today, we've seen a more than 400% increase in money going to the top as profits, compared with a rise in *household* income of around 15% (and a drop in individual income).

Since profits represent what's left over after all the other bills are paid and investments made, for profits to have risen so dramatically since roughly the Reagan years, what happened?

Why didn't all that money go, as it once did, to increases in wages so that workers were sharing in the increasing corporate prosperity they were helping create?

Monopoly plays a huge role in the answer.

How Reaganomics Killed the Jetsons

> Ms. Mornin: *That's good, because I work three jobs and I feel like I contribute.*
> President Bush: *You work three jobs?*
> Ms. Mornin: *Three jobs, yes.*
> President Bush: *Uniquely American, isn't it? I mean, that is fantastic that you're doing that.*
> —President George W. Bush, Omaha, Nebraska, Town Hall, February 2005

President George W. Bush (and President Donald Trump, who brags about low unemployment although virtually all newly created jobs are low-paying) might have thought it was "fantastic" that one of his supporters had to work three jobs to pay her family's bills, but most Americans wouldn't agree, and never have. The movement to restrict labor to 10 hours a day (from the then-widespread 14-hour day) got underway in the United States and Great Britain in the 1830s[23] and reached its peak here after the Civil War, and in England in 1847 with the passage of the Factories Act.[24]

The fight for the eight-hour day was kicked off in a big way by President Ulysses S. Grant in 1869, when he declared by proclamation that it should be the industrial standard of the United States.[25] The United Mine Workers won it in 1898, and in 1926 Henry Ford adopted it, after years of agitation by his workers. The great Flint Sit-Down Strike of 1937 caused its adoption across the auto industry and most others.

In 1980, the year before Reagan kicked off his "revolution," the 40-hour work week was standard all across America, although since then the hours that workers put in have steadily risen as the rate of unionization has fallen from around a third of all workers when Reagan was inaugurated to around 6% of the private workforce today.

But this was not the state of life for human beings during the vast majority of our history.

Back in the early 1960s, Richard Borshay Lee spent almost two years with the !Kung Bushmen in a part of what is now Botswana called Dobe. He wrote,

In all, the adults of the Dobe camp worked about two and a half days a week. Since the average working day was about six hours long, the fact emerges that !Kung Bushmen of Dobe, despite their harsh environment, devote from twelve to nineteen hours a week to getting food. Even the hardest-working individual in the camp, a man named ≠oma who went out hunting on sixteen of the twenty-eight days, spent a maximum of thirty-two hours a week in the food quest.[26]

Marshall Sahlins, in his 1974 book *Stone Age Economics*, estimated, based on the fieldwork of Lee and others, that the average hunter-gatherer worked between three and five hours a day.[27] Which *Time* magazine posited, in 1966, was where we'd be by the year 2000, a third of a century off in the future.[28]

Just a few years earlier, Hanna-Barbera had produced a cartoon show called *The Jetsons*, about a family in the future, where George Jetson, the family patriarch, worked at Spaceley's Sprockets, doing the difficult work of pushing a button every 10 minutes or so. The future was going to be, at least for working people, easier.

And, indeed, *Time* noted, "By 2000, the machines will be producing so much that everyone in the U.S. will, in effect, be independently wealthy. With Government benefits, even nonworking families will have, by one estimate, an annual income of $30,000–$40,000. How to use leisure meaningfully will be a major problem."[29]

And that was $30,000 to $40,000 in 1966 dollars, which would be roughly $199,000 to $260,000 in today's dollars.

Or, instead of taking a paycheck that was so much larger, American workers could take the same pay they already had and, like George Jetson, just push a button for three or four hours a day.

Ask anybody who was teenage or older in the 1960s: this was the big sales pitch for automation and the coming computer age. Americans looked forward to increased productivity from robots, computers, and automation translating into fewer hours worked or more pay, or both, for every American worker.

There was good logic behind the idea in 1966, because back then, that was how things actually worked.

The premise was simple. With better technology, companies would become more efficient and make more things in less time. Revenues would skyrocket, and Americans would bring home bigger and bigger paychecks, all the while working less and less. By the year 2000, *Time* posited, we would enter what was then referred to as "The Leisure Society."

Futurists speculated that the biggest problem facing America in the future would be just how the heck everyone would use all their extra leisure time!

Then came 1980.

The industrialists and financiers who helped put Reagan in office and cheered him on with their think tanks and media also saw this increased productivity coming, and with it a huge opportunity. What if all that productivity—and the extra revenue it would create—could go to them instead of to the workers?

All it would take would be to break the unions, lower top tax rates so that the money didn't end up with the government instead, and reconfigure corporate governance laws to let small- and medium-sized companies be gobbled up by giant corporations that could provide CEOs and senior executives with pay in the million-dollars-a-month to million-dollars-a-day range.

Reagan obligingly saw to it all, and right-wing think tanks and their monopolist funders have kept us there.

Reaganomics Ensured American Leisure for the Few, Not the Many

As productivity continued to rise, due to increasing automation and better technology, so too would everyone's wages. Or so went the theory. The glue holding this logic together was

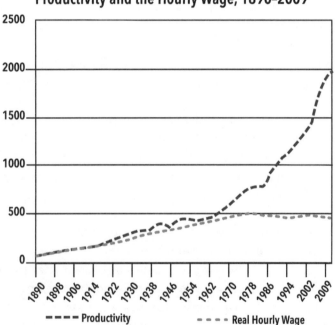

Figure 2. Productivity and the hourly wage, 1890–2009.

Sources: US Department of Labor, Bureau of Labor Statistics; US Department of the Census, after D. Hayes, *Historical Statistics of the United States* (2006). Based on a graph by Jason Ricciuti-Borenstein.

the then-top marginal income tax rate. In 1963, just before the *Time* article was written, the top marginal income tax rate was 90%. What that did was encourage CEOs to keep more money in their businesses: to invest in new technology, to pay their workers more, to hire new workers and expand.

After all, what's the point of sucking millions and millions of dollars out of your business if it's going to be taxed at 90% (or even the 70% that President Lyndon Johnson lowered it to in 1966)?

According to this line of reasoning, if businesses were suddenly to become way more profitable and efficient thanks to automation, then that money would flow throughout the business—raising everyone's standard of living and increasing everyone's leisure time, from the CEO to the janitor.

But when Reagan dropped that top tax rate down to 28%, everything changed. Now, as businesses became far more profitable, there was a far greater incentive for CEOs to pull those profits out of the company and pocket them, because they were suddenly paying an incredibly low tax rate.

And that's exactly what they did.

All those new profits, thanks to automation, that were *supposed* to go to everyone, giving us all bigger paychecks and more time off, went to the top.

Suddenly, the symmetry in the productivity/wages chart broke down. Productivity continued increasing, since technology continued improving, and revenues and profits kept increasing with it.

But wages stayed flat.

And, again, since greater and greater profits could be sucked out of the company and taxed at lower levels, there was no incentive to reduce the number of hours everyone had to work.

In the 1950s, before that *Time* magazine article predicting the Leisure Society was written, the average American working in manufacturing put in about 42 hours of work a week. Today, the average American working in manufacturing puts in about 40 hours of work a week. This means that even though productivity has increased 400% since 1950, Americans in manufacturing are working, on average, only two fewer hours a week.

If productivity is four times higher today than in 1950, then Americans should be able to work four times less, or just 10 hours a week, to afford the same 1950s lifestyle when a family of four could get by on just one paycheck, own a home, own a car, put their kids through school, take a vacation every now and then, and retire comfortably.

That's the definition of the Leisure Society: 10 hours of work a week, and the rest of the time spent with family, with travel, with creativity, with whatever you want. And if our tax laws and our corporate anti-monopoly laws that restrained the worst corporate bad behavior had stayed the same as they were in 1966, we might well be either working 10 hours a week for around $50,000 a year in income, or working 40-hour weeks for over $200,000 a year.

But all of this was washed away by the Reagan tax cuts. Those *trillions* of dollars that would have gone to workers? They went into the estates and stock portfolios of the top 1%. Combine this with Reagan's brutal crackdown on striking PATCO (Professional Air Traffic Controllers Organization) members that kicked off a three-decades-long assault on another substantial pillar of the middle class—organized labor—and life today is anything but leisurely for working people in America.

More Unequal than Rome

Instead of leisure, working people got feudalism.

From 1947 to 1981, all classes of Americans saw their incomes grow together; as a result of the Reagan tax cuts, that era ended and a new era of Reaganomics began. Since then, only the wealthiest among us have gotten rich from economic boom times.

Today, workers' wages as a percentage of GDP are at an all-time low. Yet, corporate profits as a percentage of GDP are at an all-time high.

The top 1% of Americans own 40% of the nation's wealth. In fact, just 400 Americans own more wealth than 150 million other Americans combined, and they pay lower taxes than anybody in the bottom half of American families economically.[30]

Walmart, Inc., the world's largest private employer, personifies this inequality best. It's a corporation that in 2011 gained more revenue than any other corporation in America. It raked in $16.4 billion in profits. It pays its employees minimum wage.

And the Walmart heirs, the Walton family, who occupy positions six through nine on the Forbes 400 Richest Americans list, own roughly $100 billion in wealth, which is more than the bottom 40% of Americans combined. The average Walmart employee would have to work 76 *million* 40-hour weeks to have as much wealth as one Walmart heir.

Through some interesting historical analysis, historians Walter Scheidel and Steven Friesen calculated that inequality in America today is worse than what was seen during the Roman era.[31] Thus the top 1%, just like the Roman emperors, got their Leisure Society, and they've used their financial power to capture the US government to protect their Leisure Society.

How the Monopolists Stole the US Government

Because the Founders set up America to be resistant to the coercive and corruptive influence of monopoly and vested interest, the monopolists didn't have any direct means of taking over the American government. So, two processes were necessary.

First, they knew that they'd have to take over the government. A large part of that involved the explicit capture of the third branch of government, the federal judiciary (and particularly the Supreme Court), which meant taking and holding the presidency (because the president appoints judges) at all costs, even if it required breaking the law; colluding with foreign governments, monopolies, and oligarchs; and engaging in massive election fraud, all issues addressed in previous *Hidden History* books.

Second, they knew that if they were going to succeed for any longer than a short time, they'd need popular support. This required two steps: build a monopoly-friendly intellectual and media infrastructure, and then use it to persuade people to distrust the US government.

Lewis Powell's 1971 memo kicked off the process.

Just a few months before he was nominated by President Richard Nixon to the US Supreme Court, Powell had written a memo to his good friend Eugene Sydnor Jr., the director of the US Chamber of Commerce at the time.[32] Powell's most indelible mark on the nation was not to be his 15-year tenure as a Supreme Court justice but instead that memo, which served as a declaration of war against both democracy and what he saw as an overgrown middle class. It would be a final war, a *bellum omnium contra omnes*, against everything FDR's New Deal and LBJ's Great Society had accomplished.

It wasn't until September 1972, 10 months after the Senate confirmed Powell, that the public first found out about the Powell memo (the actual written document had the word "Confidential" at the top—a sign that Powell himself hoped it would never see daylight outside of the rarified circles of his rich friends). By then, however, it had already found its way to the desks of CEOs all across the nation and was, with millions in corporate and billionaire money, already being turned into real actions, policies, and institutions.

During its investigation into Powell as part of the nomination process, the FBI never found the memo, but investigative journalist Jack Anderson did, and he exposed it in a September 28, 1972, column in the *Washington Post* titled, "Powell's Lesson to Business Aired." Anderson wrote, "Shortly before his appointment to the Supreme Court, Justice Lewis F. Powell Jr. urged business leaders in a confidential memo to use the courts as a 'social, economic, and political' instrument."[33]

Pointing out that the memo hadn't been discovered until after Powell was confirmed by the Senate, Anderson wrote,

"Senators . . . never got a chance to ask Powell whether he might use his position on the Supreme Court to put his ideas into practice and to influence the court in behalf of business interests."[34]

This was an explosive charge being leveled at the nation's rookie Supreme Court justice, a man entrusted with interpreting the nation's laws with complete impartiality. But Anderson was a true investigative journalist and no stranger to taking on American authority or to the consequences of his journalism. He'd exposed scandals from the Truman, Eisenhower, Johnson, Nixon, and Reagan administrations. In his report on the memo, Anderson wrote, "[Powell] recommended a militant political action program, ranging from the courts to the campuses."[35]

Powell's memo was both a direct response to Franklin Roosevelt's battle cry decades earlier and a response to the tumult of the 1960s. He wrote, "No thoughtful person can question that the American economic system is under broad attack."[36]

When Sydnor and the Chamber received the Powell memo, corporations were growing tired of their second-class status in America. The previous 40 years had been a time of great growth and strength for the American economy and America's middle-class workers—and a time of sure and steady increases of profits for corporations—but CEOs wanted more.

If only they could find a way to wiggle back into the minds of the people (who were just beginning to forget the monopolists' previous exploits of the 1920s), then they could get their tax cuts back; they could trash the "burdensome" regulations that were keeping the air we breathe, the water we drink, and the food we eat safe; and the banksters among them could inflate another massive economic bubble to make themselves all mind-bogglingly rich. It could, if done right, be a return to the Roaring Twenties.

But how could they do this? How could they persuade Americans to take another shot at what was widely considered a dangerous "free market" ideology and economic framework that had crashed the economy in 1929?

Lewis Powell had an answer, and he reached out to the Chamber of Commerce—the hub of corporate power in America—with a strategy. As Powell wrote, "Strength lies in organization, in careful long-range planning and implementation, in consistency of action over an indefinite period of years, in the scale of financing available only through joint effort, and in the political power available only through united action and national organizations." Thus, Powell said, "the role of the National Chamber of Commerce is therefore vital."[37]

In the nearly 6,000-word memo, Powell called on corporate leaders to launch an economic and ideological assault on college and high school campuses, the media, the courts, and Capitol Hill. The objective was simple: the revival of the royalist-controlled "free market" system. As Powell put it, "[T]he ultimate issue . . . [is the] survival of what we call the free enterprise system, and all that this means for the strength and prosperity of America and the freedom of our people."

The first front that Powell encouraged the Chamber to focus on was the education system. "[A] priority task of business—and organizations such as the Chamber—is to address the campus origin of this hostility [to big business]," Powell wrote.[38] What worried Powell was the new generation of young Americans growing up to resent corporate culture. He believed colleges were filled with "Marxist professors" and that the pro-business agenda of Harding, Coolidge, and Hoover had fallen into disrepute since the Great Depression. He knew that winning this war of economic ideology in America required spoon-feeding the next generation of leaders the doctrines of a free-market theology, from high school all the way through graduate and business school.

At the time, college campuses were rallying points for the progressive activism sweeping the nation as young people demonstrated against poverty, the Vietnam War, and in support of civil rights. Powell proposed a list of ways the Chamber could retake the higher-education system. First, create an army of corporate-friendly think tanks that could influence education. "The Chamber should consider establishing a staff of highly qualified scholars in the social sciences who do believe in the system," he wrote.[39]

Then, go after the textbooks. "The staff of scholars," Powell wrote, "should evaluate social science textbooks, especially in economics, political science and sociology. . . . This would include assurance of fair and factual treatment of our system of government and our enterprise system, its accomplishments, its basic relationship to individual rights and freedoms, and comparisons with the systems of socialism, fascism and communism."[40]

Powell argued that the civil rights movement and the labor movement were already in the process of rewriting textbooks. "We have seen the civil rights movement insist on re-writing many of the textbooks in our universities and schools. The labor unions likewise insist that textbooks be fair to the viewpoints of organized labor."[41] Powell was concerned that the Chamber of Commerce was not doing enough to stop this growing progressive influence and replace it with a pro-plutocratic perspective.

"Perhaps the most fundamental problem is the imbalance of many faculties," Powell pointed out. "Correcting this is indeed a long-range and difficult project. Yet, it should be undertaken as a part of an overall program. This would mean the urging of the need for faculty balance upon university administrators and boards of trustees."[42] As in, the Chamber needed to infiltrate university boards in charge of hiring faculty to make sure that only corporate-friendly professors were hired.

Powell's recommendations targeted high schools as well. "While the first priority should be at the college level, the trends mentioned above are increasingly evidenced in the high schools. Action programs, tailored to the high schools and similar to those mentioned, should be considered," he urged.[43]

Next, Powell turned to the media, instructing that "[r]eaching the campus and the secondary schools is vital for the long-term. Reaching the public generally may be more important for the shorter term." Powell added, "It will . . . be essential to have staff personnel who are thoroughly familiar with the media, and how most effectively to communicate with the public." He advocated that the same system "applies not merely to so-called educational programs . . . but to the daily 'news analysis' which so often includes the most insidious type of criticism of the enterprise system."

Following Powell's lead, in 1987 Reagan suspended the Fairness Doctrine (which required radio and TV stations to "program in the public interest," a phrase that was interpreted by the FCC to mean hourly genuine news on radio and quality prime-time news on TV, plus a chance for "opposing points of view" rebuttals when station owners offered on-air editorials), and then in 1996 President Bill Clinton signed the Telecommunications Act of 1996, which eliminated most media-monopoly ownership rules. That same year, billionaire Rupert Murdoch started Fox News, an enterprise that would lose hundreds of millions in its first few years but would grow into a powerhouse on behalf of the monopolists.

From Reagan's inauguration speech in 1981 to this day, the single and consistent message heard, read, and seen on conservative media, from magazines to talk radio to Fox, is that government is the cause of our problems, not the solution. "Big government" is consistently—more consistently than any other meme or theme—said to be the very worst thing that could happen to America or its people, and after a few decades, many Americans came to believe it. Reagan scaremongered from a *presidential podium* in 1986 that "the nine most terrifying words in the English language are: I'm from the government and I'm here to help."

Once the bond between people and their government was broken, the next steps were straightforward: Reconfigure the economy to work largely for the corporate and rich, reconfigure the criminal justice system to give white-collar criminals a break while hyper-punishing working-class people of all backgrounds, and reconfigure the electoral systems to ensure that conservatives get reelected.

Then use all of that to push deregulation so that they can quickly consolidate into monopolies or oligopolies.

Government as a Monopoly?

The core argument of the "government is bad" crowd is that government is, itself, a monopoly. Since everybody knows that monopolies are bad things, so, too, government must be an intolerable affront that reduces the quality of life for its citizens. This meme has been incredibly destructive to America's working people, who've become hostile to government while losing their wariness of corporate monopoly.

There's one type of monopoly that's actually good, with a single caveat. That's called a "natural monopoly," and for it to work properly, it generally *requires* government. Consider your home. While you can buy a new stove or sofa or rug from many different companies, you'll be hard-pressed to buy your water, electric, or septic from more than one single vendor. There's only one power line, water line, and sewer line attached to your home. Thus, power, water, and septic are generally referred to as "natural monopolies."

To provide the best and most reliable service at the lowest price, communities across America have opted to have public (government) ownership of these utilities. Publicly owned electric companies, for example, provide power for about 15% less than privately owned for-profit power corporations, and they do so with an average of 59 minutes of service loss per year compared with 133 minutes of lost power from for-profit companies.[44]

While public power systems saw a huge growth spurt through the 1930s (with the help of New Deal programs building huge dams and starting the Tennessee Valley Authority), '40s, '50s, and '60s, the tide turned as a neoliberal (deregulated or laissez-faire capitalism) privatization craze crept across the American landscape in a big way following the election of Reagan in 1980.

Today, only one in seven households gets its power from publicly owned companies; the rest of us are paying the extra 15% for corporate profits and shareholder dividends, and living with more outages because for-profit companies are paying dividends instead of maintaining their equipment.

This turned deadly in 2018 when wildfires erupted across California, a significant number of which were started by poorly maintained Pacific Gas & Electric power lines. Their quest for ever-increasing profits literally killed people.

As the July 10, 2019, headline and subhead in the *Wall Street Journal* noted: "PG&E Knew for Years Its Lines Could Spark Wildfires, and Didn't Fix Them: Documents obtained by the *Wall Street Journal* show that the utility has long been aware that parts of its 18,500-mile transmission system were dangerously outdated."[45]

PG&E took money devoted to updating their systems and instead passed it along to their shareholders and executives. Judge William Alsup, supervising PG&E's probation for killing eight people in a 2010 gas pipeline explosion, noted that "PG&E pumped out $4.5 billion in dividends and let the tree [trimming] budget wither." The result was a series of deadly wildfires caused by downed power lines, like the Camp Fire of 2018 that destroyed 14,000 homes and killed 85 people.[46]

Just after that 2010 explosion, it was revealed that PG&E had taken roughly $100 million that was earmarked for safety upgrades and instead distributed it, in part, to its senior executives.[47]

With the economic power derived from control of a natural monopoly, private power companies started flexing their political muscles. The legislature of Hawaii, for example, the only state to get its electricity *entirely* from private power companies, allows those companies to heavily penalize their customers who try to put solar on their homes or businesses.

The Hawaiian utility began rigorously enforcing their ability to punish solar-installing customers during the George W. Bush administration, and *Scientific American* magazine noted, "Since the Oahu rule went into effect three months ago, it has hurt business and 'deflated the movement,' [Charles] Wang [owner of a small Hawaiian solar-installation company] said. The rule led to a 50 percent drop in business in this quarter at many solar installers, according to interviews with many in Hawaii's solar industry."[48]

The article added that in 2007 there were more than 300 solar installation companies in the state, but by 2013 the number was down to "just a few dozen." Nichola Groom, the article's author, noted, "R&R Solar Supply, a 25-year-old distributor of solar panels to installers statewide, recently rented nine 40-foot containers to store panels meant to go on Hawaiian rooftops in the fourth quarter—typically the industry's busiest time of year. Its Honolulu warehouse is 'packed to the gills,' said Chief Executive Officer Rolf Christ, adding his panel business is down 50 percent."[49]

Natural monopolies in the hands of corporate hustlers are so ripe for exploitation that most states regulate the private utilities just to keep their citizens from getting repeatedly taken advantage of. And so citizens end up paying for our government to maintain a separate regulatory apparatus just to protect its citizens from rapacious private utility executives, plus paying those executives millions a year, plus a large slice of the action going to stockholders. One wonders why any community in America would go for these kinds of companies, particularly when Europe is running pell-mell toward ditching its private utilities for state-owned enterprises.

Germany is at the forefront of the movement toward *remunicipalization*, with the Transnational Institute highlighting, in 2018, 347 of the 835 Europe-wide examples of utilities being clawed back from private and into public hands happening in that country. Two hundred and eighty-four of them were in the energy sector.[50]

The thing preventing America's recovery from the international experiment with privatization during the period from 1980 to 2010 has largely been the US Supreme Court, starting with its *Buckley v. Valeo* and *First National Bank of Boston v. Bellotti* rulings in 1976 and 1978, respectively (see *The Hidden History of the Supreme Court*), and most recently *Citizens United v. FEC*, that for-profit companies and the billionaires they produce can pour unlimited amounts of money into the campaigns of the politicians that we, uniquely among developed nations, allow them to own.

Now, the same people who trust their government to correctly execute criminals, deliver their mail, and route their airline's flight safely home, as the result of Reagan's rhetoric and decades of "think tank" spokespeople appearing daily on TV and radio news shows, no longer trust government when it comes to regulating the oil and gas industry or protecting coal miners. They trust their government to get them their Social Security or tax refund check but don't think state or local governments can successfully run natural monopolies.

Commons vs. Private

Reagan's "starve the beast" strategy has been used for nearly 50 years to shrink government until it no longer works well and then point to that failure to justify privatization.

Trump most recently reduced the workforces of Social Security, the Environmental Protection Agency (EPA), the US Department of Agriculture (USDA), and the Internal Revenue Service (IRA) by tens of thousands as his contribution to starving the "beast" of government: the result is that it can now take two years for Social Security to process a disability claim; the EPA is virtually impotent against corporate polluters; the USDA is letting factory farms "self regulate," producing a nationwide explosion of food poisoning; and the IRS has largely stopped conducting large, multiyear audits of wealthy people, focusing instead on cheaper and faster audits of average working people—all while private tax-preparing companies' efforts to prevent the IRS from offering free tax services got a huge boost.

The rationale for "starve the beast" is that when things are done by private industry, they're "more efficient" and "better done" than when done by government.

I lived in Germany, right near the East-West border, in the 1980s and remember well the Trabbies, these awful little three-cylinder, two-stroke, four-passenger cars that the communist government of East Germany manufactured for its citizens. They were terrible—stinky, unreliable, and dangerous.

I don't want my car made by the government. Nor my computer, nor my clothes.

On the other hand, when we look at how Enron handled electric service in multiple states, or how Comcast and other big ISPs treat their customers, or the horrors of the private student loan industry, it's pretty hard to think that we want private industry running anything that includes the commons.

Which raises the core questions in this debate: What is the commons? Where does it begin and end?

The answers to those questions go a long way toward revealing where a person sits on the economic/political spectrum.

Those who think that the commons should be very, very narrowly defined tend to be libertarians and conservative Republicans. It's fine, in their minds, for government to take care of basic police and army functions, but even the fire department or interstate highway being publicly owned instead of being a profit center for a capitalist is a stretch too far. On the other end of the spectrum are communist governments like those in Vietnam and Cuba, where the government owns or supervises even most manufacturing and retailing (although both countries are experimenting with limited free enterprise). In the middle are most developed countries today, what many of them call democratic socialism.

In this system with both a mixed government and a mixed economy, the commons are broadly defined as those areas of the physical and economic landscape where there's broad general ownership and a large impact on the quality of life of most citizens.

Thus, a democratic socialist state would argue that water and electric are part of the commons because they're "natural monopolies," things that are hard to run competitively. We have only one water line and one electric line coming into our homes, so competition is pretty much out of the picture; turning them both over to local government, accountable to the consumers rather than distant stockholders, only makes sense.

And, indeed, across the nation, utilities that are owned and run by the government generally have a much better record of safety, service, and reasonable pricing than do privately owned utilities.

Democratic socialists extend this logic to health care and, in some cases, banking. If everybody in the country is paying for everybody else's health care via their taxes, the entire society has an incentive to behave in healthy ways. In Denmark, bicycling is so aggressively encouraged (to reduce the nation's health care costs) that about half the total traffic in Copenhagen on any given day is made up of individuals on their bikes.

In most European states and in Australia, for example, the social pressures to quit smoking come from people concerned about the public health, but also from people who know that every smoker's cancer is going to cost their society a half-million dollars, a portion of which will come out of their taxes.

Many of these nations even regulate their food supplies to discourage the consumption of obesogens (compounds contributing to obesity) like high-fructose corn syrup and some of the hormone-interrupting compounds that are used as flame retardants, as liners of tin and aluminum cans, as plasti-cizers, and to make carryout-food paper trays and coffee cups waterproof.

The problem with these types of democratic socialist sys-tems, from the point of view of libertarians and conservatives, is twofold: First, they don't philosophically fit in because they're "big government" solutions, and anything that makes government bigger is, in their minds, an intrinsic evil. Second, no good capitalist is making money on any of the commons, and that's intolerable because, they say, capitalism when applied to the commons will make the commons function better due to "market forces" and "the invisible hand."

But comparing the American health care system with that of any other of the 34 OECD "most developed countries" in the world gives the lie to the libertarian line. Every other devel-oped country in the world has some sort of universal health care program, and all of them deliver health care as good as or better than America's, at anywhere from two-thirds to half the cost of what Americans pay.

When the commons are sliced and diced by private enter-prise, the result is almost always a true "tragedy of the com-mons" (to quote ecologist Garrett Hardin): exploitation, monopoly, and price gouging.

Whether in a nation's schools, its utilities, its prisons, its public roads, or even its internet access, when these core parts of the commons are privatized and then ring-fenced by private enterprise, somebody is going to get rich, and the majority of the people will be poorer.

Libertarians Object

Libertarians and their fellow travelers, however, deny that such natural monopolies even exist.

"There is no evidence at all that at the outset of public-utility regulation there existed any such phenomenon as a 'natural monopoly,'" wrote Thomas J. DiLorenzo for the *Review of Austrian Economics*.[51] He opened the article, in fact, with an even bolder statement by libertarian apologist Murray Rothbard: "The very term 'public utility' . . . is an absurd one."

Libertarianism was invented in 1946 by a think tank organized to advance the interests of very big business, the Foundation for Economic Education. FEE's project was to provide a pseudoscientific and pseudoeconomic rationale for business's attacks on government regulation, particularly government "interfering" in "markets" by protecting organized labor's right to form a union. They invented the libertarian movement out of whole cloth to accomplish this.

FEE was founded in 1946 by Donaldson Brown, a member of the boards of directors of General Motors and DuPont, along with his friend Leonard Read, a senior US Chamber of Commerce executive (and failed businessman).

In 1950, the US House Select Committee on Lobbying Activities, sometimes called the Buchanan Committee after its chairman, Representative Frank Buchanan, D-Pa., found that FEE was funded by the nation's three largest oil companies, US Steel, the Big Three automakers, the three largest retailers in the country, the nation's largest chemical companies, and other industrial and banking giants like GE, Eli Lilly, and Merrill Lynch.

As reporter Mark Ames found when researching the Buchanan Committee's activities, FEE's board of directors included Robert Welch, who would go on to found the John Birch Society with help from Fred Koch, along with a well-known racist and anti-Semite, J. Reuben Clark, and Herb Cornuelle, who was also on the board of United Fruit (which was then running operations against working and indigenous people in Hawaii and Central America).[52]

The Buchanan Committee also discovered that an obscure University of Chicago economist, Milton Friedman, was working as a paid shill for the real estate industry. He was hired through FEE to come up with and publicize "economic" reasons for ending rent price controls, commonly known as *rent control*. The public good didn't matter, Friedman concluded; all that mattered was the ability of businessmen to work in a "free market"—free of any substantive obligation to anything other than their own profits.

The Buchanan Committee knew what it had found. It reported the following:

> *It is difficult to avoid the conclusion that the Foundation for Economic Education exerts, or at least expects to exert, a considerable influence on national legislative policy...*
> *. It is equally difficult to imagine that the nation's largest corporations would subsidize the entire venture if they did not anticipate that it would pay solid, long-range legislative dividends.*

As Ames notes and the committee uncovered, "'Libertarianism' was a project of the corporate lobby world, launched as a big business 'ideology' in 1946 by the US

Chamber of Commerce and the National Association of Manufacturers."[53]

The man financing much of this, Herbert Nelson, head of the real estate lobby, didn't think that democracy was even particularly useful, especially if it interfered with the ability of very wealthy people and big corporations to control both markets and the nation. As Nelson wrote, and the committee revealed, "I do not believe in democracy. I think it stinks. I don't think anybody except direct taxpayers should be allowed to vote."

In that, Nelson was simply echoing the perspective of many of the conservative movement's most influential thinkers, from Ayn Rand to Phyllis Schlafly. Ask any objectivist (follower of Ayn Rand) or true libertarian, and they'll tell you up front: the markets, not voters in a democracy, should determine the fate and future of a nation.

As Stephen Moore, whom Donald Trump tried to nominate to the Federal Reserve, told me on my radio program during the Bush years, he considers capitalism more important than democracy. There's only one power on earth that can successfully take on monopolists who want to dominate not only a nation's markets but its politics as well: government. Only We the People can challenge the power of massive, aggregated wealth and the political power it carries.

That's why libertarians and their libertarian-influenced Republican allies constantly rail against government. As Reagan said in his 1981 inaugural address: "Government is not the solution to our problem; government is the problem." And if you own a major oil refinery that's facing huge fines for polluting and causing cancers and don't want to spend the money to clean it up, that's true.

Using libertarian theory and theology, big business now has an army of true believers, ready to join the newest billionaire-funded Tea Party to complain about things like health and safety regulations by calling them "government health insurance" and "government interference."

Meanwhile, it's now fashionable for tech billionaires to call themselves libertarians.[54]

The New Feudalism

The war for the heart and soul of America, funded by libertarian billionaires, has moved into the press, the internet, and our political arena. In that struggle, it's more accurate to portray libertarians as "feudalists" than as advocates of anything new.

Feudalism doesn't exclusively refer to a point in time or history when streets were filled with mud and people lived as peasants. More broadly, it refers to an economic and political *system*, just like democracy or communism or socialism or theocracy.

The biggest difference is that instead of power being held by the people, the government, or the church, those who own property and the other necessities of life hold power. At its essential core, feudalism could be defined as "government of, by, and for the rich."[55]

Marc Bloch is one of the great 20th-century scholars of the feudal history of Europe. In his book *Feudal Society*, he points out that in almost every case, with both European feudalism and feudalism in China, South America, and Japan, "feudalism coincided with a profound weakening of the State, particularly in its protective capacity."[56]

Given most accepted definitions of feudalism, feudal societies can't emerge in nations with a strong social safety net and a proactive government. But when the wealthiest in a society seize government and then weaken it so that it can't represent the interests of the people, the transition has begun into a new era of feudalism. "European feudalism should therefore be seen as the outcome of the dissolution of older societies," Bloch says.

Whether the power and wealth agent that takes the place of government is a local baron, lord, king, or corporation, if it has greater power in the lives of individuals than does a representative government, the nation has dissolved into feudalism.

Bluntly, Bloch states, "The feudal system meant the rigorous economic subjection of a host of humble folk to a few powerful men."[57] This doesn't mean the end of government but, instead, the subordination of government to the interests of the feudal lords. Interestingly, even in feudal Europe, Bloch points out, "[t]he concept of the State never absolutely disappeared, and where it retained the most vitality men continued to call themselves 'free.'"[58]

The transition from a governmental society to a feudal one is marked by the rapid accumulation of power and wealth in a few hands, with a corresponding reduction in the power and responsibilities of government. Once the rich and powerful gain control of the government, they turn it upon itself, usually first radically reducing their own taxes, while raising taxes on the middle class and poor. Says Bloch: "Nobles need not pay *taille* [taxes]."

Bringing this to today, consider that in 1982, just before the first Reagan-Bush "supply side" tax cut, the average wealth of the Forbes 400 was $200 million. Just four years later, their average wealth had more than doubled to over $500 million each, aided by massive tax cuts.

Today, as the Institute for Policy Studies notes, "With a combined worth of $2.34 trillion, the Forbes 400 [individuals] own more wealth than the bottom 61 percent of the country combined, a staggering 194 million people."[59] *Forbes* magazine, for 2017, reported, "The minimum net worth to make The Forbes 400 list of richest Americans is now a record $2 billion. . . . [T]he average net worth rose to $6.7 billion."[60]

While the Forbes 400 richest Americans have gone from an average wealth of $200 million in 1982 to over $6 billion today, the average wealth of working Americans stayed flat, in the face of explosions in the costs of health, education, and housing.

Median household wealth in 2013, for example, was $81,000—about the same as in 1983 (the first year of household wealth surveys by the federal government).[61] But the median price of a house in 1983—around $74,000 (or $180,000 in today's dollars[62])—has, according to the US Census Bureau, risen to over $220,000 today (and it's massively higher in most cities).[63] In 1983, the average person working a minimum wage job could afford a college education; now there's over $1.7 trillion in student debt.

And in 2017, Trump and his GOP doubled down on their plan to move America from democracy to feudal oligarchy by cutting more than $1.5 *trillion* in taxes, most of the cuts directed to the uber-rich and giant monopolistic corporations. As a result, massive companies like Amazon, Chevron, General Motors, Delta, Halliburton, and IBM paid *nothing* in federal income taxes the next year.

In every sector of our economy, big businesses have been concentrating power since the 1980s, and America's once-strong middle class has been crushed under their heels.

From Route 66 to Anytown, USA

While the cancerous growth of giant corporate monopolies and oligopolies was largely held in check from the time of FDR until the Reagan administration, America's middle class began to feel the influence of the laissez-faire Chicago School of Economics and Robert Bork in the last years of Nixon's presidency. During Nixon's era, when the US economy was about a third the size it is now, there were about twice as many publicly traded companies as there are today.

Public companies began to collapse in earnest in the mid-1990s, as the Clinton administration embraced neoliberal economics and maintained Reagan's policy of not seriously enforcing the Sherman Antitrust Act. In 1996, there were roughly 8,000 publicly traded companies; today it's in the neighborhood of 4,000.[64]

In my lifetime, America has transformed from a nation of small and local family businesses into a nation of functional monopolies where small handfuls, typically three to five giant companies, control around 80% of pretty much every industry and marketplace, and make pricing and other decisions in concert with each other.

We see this clearly in industries like airlines and pharmaceuticals, but it exists in pretty much every industry in America of any consequence. It's often obscured, because companies operate under dozens or even hundreds of brand names, and they rarely list on their packaging or advertising the name of the corporate behemoth that owns them.

As Jonathan Tepper pointed out in *The Myth of Capitalism*, fully 90% of the beer that Americans drink is controlled by two companies.[65] Air travel is mostly controlled by four companies, and over half of the nation's banking is done by five banks. In multiple states there are only one or two health insurance companies, high-speed internet is in a near-monopoly state virtually everywhere in America (75% of us can "choose" only one company), and three companies control around three-quarters of the entire pesticide and seed markets. The vast majority of radio and TV stations in the country are owned by a small handful of companies, and the internet is dominated by Google and Facebook.

Right now, 10 giant corporations control, either directly or indirectly, virtually every consumer product we buy. Kraft, Coca-Cola, PepsiCo, Nestlé, Procter & Gamble, General Mills, Kellogg's, Mars, Unilever, and Johnson & Johnson together have a stranglehold on the American consumer. You can pick just about any industry in America and see the same monopolistic characteristics.

A study published in November 2018 by Jan De Loecker, Jan Eeckhout, and Gabriel Unger showed that as companies have gotten bigger and bigger, squashing their small and medium-sized competitors, they've used their increased market power to fatten their own bottom lines rather than develop new products or do things helpful to their communities or employees. Much of this shows up in increased profit margins, the benefits of which are passed along to shareholders and executives, rather than consumers.

They note that, "while aggregate markups were more or less stable between 1955 and 1980, there has been a steady rise since 1980, from 21% above cost to 61% above cost in 2016."

Markups (the price charged above production costs), they note, were fairly constant between the 1950s and the 1980s, but there was a sharp increase starting in 1980. Thus, they conclude, "[i]n 2016, the average markup charged is 61% over marginal cost, compared to 21% in 1980."

Markups, of course, define what'll be left over for profits and dividends.

Additionally, everywhere the size of companies and the domination of the market have increased, so have markups.[66]

For most of the history of our nation—and even the centuries before the American Revolution—one dimension of "the American Dream" was to start a small local business like a cleaners, clothing store, hotel, restaurant, hardware store, or theater, and then not only run it for the rest of your life but be able to pass it along to your children and grandchildren.

The first four years of the 1960s saw a new TV show—first in black-and-white and then in color—starring Martin Milner and George Maharis. The two drove on the nation's most well-known highway, Route 66, every week, stopping in small towns and mixing it up with the locals.

In the trailer for the classic DVD set of the show, Maharis asks Milner, "How many guys do you know that have knocked around as much as we have, and still made it pay?"

"Oh, we sure make it pay," Milner replies. "Almost lynched in Gareth, drowned in Grand Isle, and beat up in New Orleans . . ."

I still remember being fascinated as a nine-year-old by the geographic, cultural, and linguistic diversity of the towns they visited across my nation. Every town was unique and was generally identified by the local businesses, which often provided a job for a few days for Tod and Buz.

Today, by contrast, you could be dropped from an airplane from a few miles up and land in any city in America unable to figure out where you were. Instead of the Peoria Diner, it's Olive Garden or Ruby Tuesday. Instead of the Lansing Hotel, it's the Marriott. Instead of local stores named after local families, it's a few chains we all recognize or Amazon who's providing the goods Americans want.

And as industries become more and more consolidated, the predictable result is that profit margins increase, prices increase, and the quality of products and services declines. We see this most obviously in the quality of services and products from internet service providers and airlines, but it even applies to industries as eclectic as hospitals.

In 2012, the Robert Wood Johnson Foundation did an exhaustive review of studies on what's happened in the hospital business as hospitals have undergone a rapid period of consolidation since the 1990s. They concluded that the results were higher prices and stable or reduced quality of care without any reduction in costs, and that in the parts of the country where hospitals had not consolidated, care was better than in areas where it had. They found this was true of both the US and UK hospital marketplaces.[67]

But didn't we outlaw functional monopolies like this with the Sherman Antitrust Act back in 1890? And if so, what was the legal rationale for all this consolidation, and what did it have to do with Robert Bork?

The Borking of America

In 40 short years, America has devolved from being a relatively open market economy and a functioning democracy into a largely monopolistic economy and a monopolist-friendly political system. One of the principal architects of that transformation was Robert Bork.

Most Americans, if they remember Robert Bork at all, remember him as the guy who railed against homosexuality and "forced integration" in such extreme language that his nomination to the Supreme Court by Ronald Reagan had to be withdrawn. But Bork's most important effort—one he worked on for more than 15 years nearly full-time—was in reshaping the business landscape of this country.

Attending the University of Chicago, Bork took a class in antitrust from an acolyte of Milton Friedman's, Aaron Director. Bork described the class as a "religious conversion" that changed his "entire view of the world."[68] After graduation, he continued working with Director as a research associate for Director's "Antitrust Project" and repeatedly gushed about Director in his book The Antitrust Paradox, which is credited (at least by Wikipedia) for nearly singlehandedly changing America's antitrust laws.

When, in the 1970s, Chilean dictator Augusto Pinochet's private police force and army were taking democracy advocates up in helicopters and dropping them out from 3,000 feet over the Atlantic, Milton Friedman and his Chicago School boys enthusiastically signed up to help "reinvent" his economy. (A bizarre article in the libertarian magazine Reason argued, "Yes, it's true—Friedman gave advice to Pinochet. But it wasn't about how to find the best place at sea to dump the bodies of murdered political enemies."[69])

When the Soviet Union fell in the 1990s, Friedman's men advised Russia on how to privatize its economy, doing so in a way that predictably produced both oligarchy and monopoly.

As long as Pinochet privatized Chile's social security system for the benefit of that country's bankers, and Russia sold off state-owned property to increase "privately owned wealth," it was all good with Friedman and most of his associates.[70]

Bork argued, in one of the most influential essays (and, later, a book) of the 20th century, that the role of government relative to monopoly wasn't to prevent any single company from getting so large that it could crush any competitor and capture the government that was meant to regulate it. The role of antimonopoly regulation was definitely not, he reasoned, even to promote competition.

It was, instead, all about "consumer welfare," a term that he had brought into common usage and the Chicago School boys quickly picked up. In essence, he argued, it didn't matter where a product was produced or sold, or by whom; all that mattered was the price the consumer paid. As long as that price was low, all was good with the world.

It sounded so Ralph Nader-ish.

Bork was a brilliant writer and used vivid imagery to make his points. "Anti-free-market forces now have the upper hand and are steadily broadening and consolidating their victory," he wrote in "The Crisis in Antitrust," published in 1965 in the *Columbia Law Review* and cowritten with Ward S. Bowman Jr.[71] They "threaten within the foreseeable future to destroy the antitrust laws as guarantors of a competitive economy."

Having staked out his position as the advocate of antitrust, he noted that the forces that he opposed had a "real hostility toward the free market," which could be found "in the courts, in the governmental enforcement agencies, and in the Congress."

Since the 1890 Sherman Antitrust Act, America's political and judicial systems had embraced antitrust, Bork noted, so much so that in 1978 "they [antitrust doctrines] enjoy nearly universal acceptance," although "these doctrines in their present form are inadequate theoretically and seriously disruptive when applied to practical business relationships. . . .

"One may begin to suspect that antitrust," he wrote, "is less a science than an elaborate mythology, that it has operated for years on hearsay and legends rather than on reality." In fact, Bork wrote, the entire notion of antitrust law as a vehicle to protect small and local businesses from large and national predators was a terrible mistake.

Trying to stop "a [market] trend toward a more concentrated condition" is a blunder, Bork said, because "the existence of the trend is prima facie evidence that greater concentration is socially desirable. The trend indicates that there are emerging efficiencies or economies of scale . . . which make larger size more efficient." The current theory of antitrust, he noted, is "unsophisticated, but currently ascendant."

Bork argued for the Walmartification of America, saying, "It would be hard to demonstrate that the independent druggist or groceryman is any more solid and virtuous a citizen than the local manager of a chain operation. The notion that such persons are entitled to special consideration by the state is an ugly demand for class privilege."

He condemned "vague philosophizing by courts that lack the qualifications and the mandate to behave as philosopher kings. . . . [T]he system hardly deserves the name law."

In Bork's mind, when dozens of small companies are bought up by one large monopolistic company and their redundant R&D, HR, sales, and promotion/advertising departments are consolidated, laying off thousands of workers, that's a *good* thing.

"If it now takes fewer salesmen and distribution personnel to move a product from the factory to the consumer than it used to; if advertising or promotion can be accomplished less expensively, that is a net gain to society. We are all richer to that extent. Multiply such additions to social wealth by hundreds and thousands of transactions and an enormously important social phenomenon is perceived. . . . To inhibit the creation of efficiency . . . is to impose a tax upon efficiency for the purpose of subsidizing the inept."

In a particularly eloquent paragraph, he compared large companies buying up or killing off smaller competitors through predatory practices as "an evolutionary process." After all, "[t]he business equivalents of dodoes, the dinosaurs, and the great ground sloths are in for a bad time—and they should be."

To say that Bork's paper (and numerous others, and 15 years of work advocating this position) changed America would be a dramatic understatement. As he himself pointed out in his paper, in the 1962 antitrust case of *Brown Shoe Co. v. United States*, the Supreme Court blocked the merger of Brown and G. R. Kinney, two shoe manufacturers, because the combination of the two would have captured about 5% of the US shoe market. (For comparison, Nike today has 18% of the US shoe market.[72])

When Robert Bork said that the only thing that mattered was the price to the consumer, he never considered the value of good food freshly made in a local restaurant as opposed to things arriving from across the country in giant plastic boxes to chain restaurants; he never considered the value of a hardware store or a bookstore or clothing store or furniture store that would go out of its way to look through all the hundreds of suppliers to find exactly what you wanted and make sure you knew when it was available.

He never considered the importance of the local hotel and the local restaurant and the local five and dime and the local bank and 50 other local businesses all operating in a single cycle of local cash, each supporting all the others and all the others supporting each one.

He never considered new entrepreneurial opportunities for small and medium-sized businesses. He never considered keeping money within local economies. He never considered the impact on a community now having no say in how destructively businesses in that community were run. He never considered the impact on workers of giant employers engaging in nationwide union-busting and pension-stripping.

He never considered how many locally owned businesses would be wiped out when giant chains moved in and undercut their prices while also undercutting the local wage floor. He never considered how massive political power—growing from overwhelming economic/market power—would distort democracy from the level of town governance all the way up to the US Congress and the White House.

All Robert Bork thought about was low prices, because that's all he knew. And that's what he brought America.

The Fortunes Bork Made

Bork was Richard Nixon's solicitor general and acting attorney general and had a substantial impact on the thinking in the Reagan White House—so much so that Reagan rewarded his years of hard work on behalf of America's monopolists with a lifetime appointment to the federal bench in the DC Circuit, frequently a launching pad for the Supreme Court.

In the years following Lewis Powell's 1971 memo, as numerous "conservative" and "free market" think tanks and publications grew in power and funding, Bork's ideas gained wide circulation in circles of governance, business, and the law.

In 1977, in the case of *Continental T.V., Inc. v. GTE Sylvania*,[73] the Supreme Court took up Bork's idea and, for the first time in a big way, embraced the "welfare of the consumer" and "demonstrable economic effect" doctrines that Bork had been promoting for over a decade.

Neither of those phrases exists in any antitrust law, at least in Bork's context. Nonetheless, the Supreme Court embraced Bork's notion that the sole metric by which to judge monopolistic behavior should be prices that consumers pay, rather than the ability of businesses to compete or the political power that a corporation may amass.

When Ronald Reagan entered the White House in 1981, bringing with him Bork's free market philosophy and a crew from the Chicago School, he ordered the Federal Trade Commission to effectively stop enforcing antitrust laws even within the feeble guidelines that the Supreme Court had written into law in *GTE Sylvania*.

The result was an explosion of mergers-and-acquisitions activity that continues to this day, as industry after industry concentrated down to two, three, four, or five major players who function as cartels. (A brilliant blow-by-blow cataloging of that decade is found in Barry C. Lynn's book *Cornered: The New Monopoly Capitalism and the Economics of Destruction*.)

Bork's reasoning—that antitrust law should defend only the consumer (through low prices), and not workers, society, democracy, or local communities—has become such conventional wisdom that in the 2014 Supreme Court case of *FTC v. Actavis*, Chief Justice John Roberts wrote a virtual word-for-word parroting of Bork: "The point of antitrust law is to encourage competitive markets to promote consumer welfare."

Barak Orbach, professor of law at the University of Arizona, is one of a small number of scholars today who are genuine experts in the field of antitrust law. In a 2014 paper published by the American Bar Association, he wondered if Bork knew he was lying when he wrote that the authors of the Sherman Antitrust Act intended to reduce prices to advance "consumer welfare," instead of protecting the competitiveness of small and local businesses, and the independence of government at all levels.

His conclusion, in "Was the 'Crisis in Antitrust' a Trojan Horse?" was that Bork was probably just blinded by ideology and had never bothered to go back and read the *Congressional Record*, which, he noted, says nothing of the kind.[74]

While Bork wrote that "the policy the courts were intended [by the Sherman Antitrust Act] to apply is the maximization of wealth or consumer want satisfaction," Orbach said,

Members of Congress . . . were determined to take action against the trusts to stop wealth transfers from the public."

So much for that: today the Walton (Walmart) family is the richest in America and one of the richest in the world. They're worth more than $100 billion, having squirreled away more wealth than the bottom 40% of all Americans. And they spend prodigiously on right-wing political causes, from the national to the local.

Amazon's Jeff Bezos is now wealthier than any Walton; with a registered net worth of $112 *billion*, he is the richest single person in the world. Bezos is so rich that when he divorced his wife, MacKenzie Bezos, she received 19.7 million shares of Amazon worth $36.8 billion. She instantly became the world's third-richest woman, and Jeff Bezos remained the world's wealthiest man.[75] While local newspapers are shutting down or being gobbled up all over the country, Bezos personally purchased the 140-year-old *Washington Post* in 2013 for $250 million. Now Bezos, like the Walton family, can use his substantial wealth to obtain political ends that protect his wealth and allow Amazon to continue to grow.

Monopoly Is Anti-business

No matter how much Robert Bork and his colleagues say they're "pro-business," what they're actually advocating is helpful only to a very small class of very large businesses and the very wealthy people who own them or their stock. Small and medium-sized businesses, entrepreneurs, workers, communities, and start-ups are badly damaged by the focus of antitrust law being kept entirely on prices that consumers pay.

Bork—and indeed his entire class of Chicago School economists—was always focused on the interests of straight, white, wealthy men to the exclusion of women, communities of color, and people who were not the "makers" and "job creators" of their lore.

Consistent with that focus, whether applied to micro- or macroeconomics, to regulating pollution or monopolies, to their complaints about "anti-war hippies" "urban dwellers," or "women's libbers," Bork and his friends managed to insert into the political and economic bloodstream of our nation the cancer-causing virus of "greed is good" ideology. Its impact has been devastating.

In the decades prior to Reagan adopting Bork's pseudoreligion of "freedom" for the biggest corporations and richest people, the working class was growing in economic and political power just as fast as the very wealthy. Post-Reagan, their power was stripped away, and trillions of dollars of working-class wealth have been redistributed to the top 1%.

Prior to Reagan adopting Bork's notion of antitrust, there were twice as many public corporations as today, and local communities were rich with locally and family-owned businesses. Post-Reagan American towns and cities are frighteningly homogeneous, all their commercial activity having been subsumed by a handful of large national brands from groceries to gasoline to hotels to restaurants to retail.

Even niche businesses like investment advisers, car repair shops, insurance companies, hardware stores, and flower shops have been wiped out by giant national firms.

Although Reagan sold us Bork's ideas as "pro-business," in fact they were (and are) radically anti-business. By damaging the middle class, they've eviscerated what economists call "aggregate demand," the wage-driven purchases made by working-class people that drive the economy, leading to a flattening of GDP growth decade over decade.

By damaging the ability of workers to unionize, Chicago School theories have torn apart communities of laborers who once worked hand-in-glove with business to achieve mutual success.

By allowing the virtual monopolization of industry after industry, Bork's theories have decimated innovation and competition.

At their core, the way that America and, sadly, much of the rest of the world have adopted Chicago School theories has been deeply and profoundly anti-business and has badly damaged America's small businesses and middle class.

PART THREE

Living Monopoly Today and in Praise of Inefficiency

The popular mind is agitated with problems that may disturb social order, and among them all none is more threatening than the inequality of condition, of wealth, and opportunity that has grown within a single generation out of the concentration of capital into vast combinations to control production and trade and to break down competition.

**–Senator John Sherman, 1890,
speaking of his Sherman Antitrust Act**

Monopoly in Milk:
The End of a Family Dairy Farm

An older Kentucky dairy farmer named Guy Coombs described dairy farming in the 21st century to an NBC documentary crew. He told them, "It's been real rough mentally, more than physically. Feed man called me one day and said, 'How ya doin?' I said 'Physically I'm fine, mentally I wanna shoot someone.' . . . Dairy farming has been important to us. I guess we've made it a way of life, or it's been our life; we've worked hard to make a living, and we've done pretty good for well over 60 years."[1]

Now, Guy Coombs and his son have retired from the dairy milk business. They are among a hundred farmers who lost their contracts—and their livelihoods—in large part because of a shrewd business decision by one of America's behemoth retail corporations: Walmart.

The senior vice president of sourcing strategy for Walmart U.S., Tony Airoso, explained to a *USA Today* reporter in 2018, "By operating our own plant and working directly with the dairy supply chain in the Midwest, we'll further reduce operating costs and pass those savings on to our customers so that they can save money."[2]

The reasoning echoes Robert Bork's fight to allow monopolies to form in order to guarantee low prices and "consumer welfare."

But milk prices were already so low as to be pressing smaller dairy farmers out of business. Farmers who were able to remain in business relied on exclusive bulk contracts like the one that Walmart's previous supplier, Dean Foods, had with more than 100 farmers in eight states, including the Coombs family.

Walmart may be able to deliver even lower prices for consumers, but its decision to take on milk processing also has had ripple effects in the economy far beyond the prices that consumers see in stores. Walmart's milk-processing plant provides milk for more than 600 stores, and Walmart has famously squeezed out smaller alternative grocers in many places across the country. That means that Walmart is the exclusive bulk buyer and retail distributor for milk (and many other products) in many rural areas across America.

Walmart has built a massive milk-processing plant in Indiana and cut out several suppliers like Dean Foods. Those suppliers in turn canceled their contracts with family farms like the Coombses'.

The Coombses were left with no processors to buy their milk and no way to do it themselves. And so, in the third generation of the farm, the Coombses were forced to sell off their cows to slaughter.

Worse yet, the Coombses' farm wasn't paid off, so they were forced to immediately try to repurpose it just to eke out enough income to keep the bank from seizing it, and with it their house and livelihoods.

In my home state of Michigan, one reporter noted, "[s]ince 2016, it's been difficult for most dairy farmers to cover 100% of their cost of production."[3] Low prices and monopolistic purchasing power have already stressed dairy farmers, forcing them to choose between leaving the business or burning through their home's and generational equity.

The same pressures are happening across all sectors of agriculture.

For instance, just three suppliers—Tyson, Koch Foods, and Perdue Farms—control 90% of the $30 billion broiler chicken market. The result, as the *Chicago Tribune* reported in 2018, is that retailers saw a "roughly 50 percent increase in the price of broiler chickens" at wholesale.[4] This meant the retailers would have to cut their workers' wages to stay in business.

Market concentration and monopolies aren't just bad for consumers and small businesses—when it comes to our food supply, having a diverse array of producers minimizes the number of people put at risk if any one supplier has contamination issues.

The pressures of globalized supply chains and the control that behemoth retailers like Walmart and Amazon (which owns Whole Foods) exert over those supply chains mean that generations-old family farms are being gobbled up, forced into exclusive contracts, or simply pressed out of business.

Big Ag Mergers

In a 2019 *HuffPost* interview, Senator Bernie Sanders (I-Vt.) explained to Amanda Terkel the scope of the problem and what kind of action the problem requires from the American government: "[I]ncreasing concentration is true in pork, it's true in beef, it's true in chicken," Sanders said. "It's true in soybeans. And the answer is, you gotta break them up. . . . I think we've not only got to have that moratorium, but we have to go further."[5]

A moratorium on mergers in the agriculture sector would pause the problem, but it would fail to address the current overconcentration of agriculture. As in other overly concentrated sectors, the first major solution that should be implemented is to enforce antitrust laws across every sector of agriculture.

Beyond that, we need to remove the hurdles for family farmers to band together in regional co-ops that could compete at scale with larger capital-intensive farms, and which would also provide regions with a relative measure of food security, independent of global supply chains.

Monopoly in Pharma: Big Private Profits from Publicly Granted Patents

In 1923, the patent for insulin was sold for $1 to the University of Toronto. Less than 100 years later, a 26-year-old Minneapolis man named Alec Raeshawn Smith died of diabetic ketoacidosis. Alec died three days before payday, his insulin injector empty and his blood sugar at a lethal level.

How did this happen?

Until a few years after World War I, no one had figured out how to synthesize or extract insulin in a way that humans could use it, and type 1 diabetes was all but a death sentence.

Then, in the early 1920s, a team of researchers at the University of Toronto discovered a process to extract and purify insulin. The discovery saved millions of lives and earned a Nobel Prize for two of the researchers in 1923—Dr. Frederick Banting and John Macleod. The researchers patented insulin as US Patent No. 1469994 on October 9, 1923—and they quickly sold the patent to the University of Toronto for $1.

That's not a typo. These researchers had the opportunity to become unbelievably wealthy with the patent on insulin—sure, a few million people may not have been able to afford insulin and might've died between 1921 and now—but the profits from insulin would've ensured that they'd never have to see the huddled, dying masses.

Instead, the researchers sold the patent to the university for $1 so that insulin could be made widely available and millions of lives could be saved.

So why is Alec Smith dead?

Just Three Companies

That's how many companies produce and sell insulin: Sanofi of France, Novo Nordisk of Denmark, and Eli Lilly Company in the United States. It's not a true monopoly, because there are three companies, all competing for the same customers.

Together, the three companies dominate 99% of the insulin market in the United States.[6] According to a 2018 report from Prescient & Strategic Intelligence, the insulin market is expected to climb to $70.6 billion by 2023, up from an estimated $42.9 billion in 2017.[7]

According to the report, the factors driving growth in the human insulin market are "[i]ncreasing population exposure to key risk factors leading to diabetes, technological advancements in insulin delivery devices, growth in the number of diabetic patients, and [a] growing geriatric population."[8]

In other words, three companies are going to continue to rake in massive profits because the global population is getting sicker and older, and insulin-delivery devices are getting more elaborate. But none of that has anything to do with the cost of *insulin* itself.

So why has the cost of insulin doubled and even tripled over the last 20 years? Carolyn Y. Johnson of the *Washington Post* reported in 2016, "A version of insulin that carried a list price of $17 a vial in 1997 is priced at $138 [in 2016]. Another that launched two decades ago with a sticker price of $21 a vial has been increased to $255."[9]

The reality is simple: the producers of insulin care only about increasing profits.

Take Eli Lilly. As Universities Allied for Essential Medicines (UAEM) director Merith Basey explained, "This generic drug has been around for almost 100 years, yet the leading cause of death for a child with Type 1 diabetes in 2017 remains a lack of insulin.

"Globally," she continued, "one in two people with diabetes lack access. Eli Lilly was a mom-and-pop company when it entered into an agreement with the University of Toronto in 1922. Now it's part of a global monopoly."[10]

And it behaves like it.

During Alex Azar's five-year tenure as president of Eli Lilly, for instance, the price of one insulin product more than tripled. In 2012, when Azar joined Eli Lilly, the company sold an insulin product called Humalog for $74 per vial. By the time Donald Trump nominated Azar to be secretary of health and human services in 2017, Humalog cost $269 per vial.

As Alexander Zaitchik wrote in the *American Prospect* in 2017, "Humalog's $74 sticker price when Azar became CEO was already outrageous compared with other developed countries. In Sweden, a vial of the same medicine is reimbursed at the (still profitable) price of $18.38."[11]

The price increases had absolutely nothing to do with climbing manufacturing costs or expanding markets or climbing costs of research and development. The price increases happened only because three companies control 99% of the market in the United States, and higher prices mean higher profits for all of them. Three insulin producers have created a cartel situation, and the end effect is that patients in America are treated like renters in Monopoly. The insulin producers have divvied up the board, and with every property in their pockets, they've raised prices in lockstep.

As Kasia Lipska wrote in the *New York Times* in 2016, "[T]he big three have simultaneously hiked their prices. From 2010 to 2015, the price of Lantus (made by Sanofi) went up by 168 percent; the price of Levemir (made by Novo Nordisk) rose by 169 percent; and the price of Humulin R U-500 (made by Eli Lilly) soared by 325 percent."[12]

Alec Smith died because he couldn't afford his insulin, and his insulin was made unaffordable by a monopolistic global insulin cartel.

Hospital Consolidation Kills

Cindy Anderson predicted that hospital consolidation in rural Missouri would kill people. At the time, she didn't realize that her husband, Butch, would be one of its victims.

The first big wave of hospital consolidations happened in the wake of Reagan stopping enforcement of the Sherman Antitrust Act in the 1980s and ran through the late 1990s. The second wave followed when the Affordable Care Act—written with plenty of input from the hospital industry—introduced more incentives to form monopolies in 2013.

Thus, while there were 1,412 hospital mergers between 1998 and 2015, 561 of them happened in just the 2010 to 2015 period.

The National Council on Compensation Insurance (NCCI) did a deep dive into the industry in 2018 and concluded that hospital mergers "can lead to operating cost reductions for acquired hospitals of 15%–30%" while increasing "the average price of hospital services by 6%–18%."[13]

As the number of hospitals shrinks—more than 150 rural hospitals have closed just since 2005—competition decreases, the number of people employed by hospitals falls, and prices (and profits) go up.

NCCI's study found that there was not a single credible research study in America as of 2018 that showed that hospital mergers would improve "quality, access, or cost." Instead, the organization found, "[m]ergers increase the likelihood of intensive surgery and total number of surgeries, but do not improve patient outcomes." While mergers do "reduce hospital costs," they noted, they do not "reduce the price of hospital care."

In December 2019, Chris McGreal, a reporter for the *Guardian*, told the story of Cindy Anderson, who'd worked for 39 years at the Twin Rivers Hospital in rural Kennett, Missouri.[14] The hospital had been acquired by Community Health Systems, which had just built a brand-new hospital 50 miles up the road in Poplar Bluff.

The Twin Rivers Hospital was making a profit—around $5 million in its last year of operation—but the CHS corporation apparently figured that shutting it down would drive people to its newer and more efficient hospital an hour away, lifting the new hospital into profitability. Increasing ambulance time to rural communities for emergencies like heart attacks, strokes, and car accidents didn't appear to show up in their calculations.

When Twin Rivers was still open, Cindy's husband, Butch, had a heart attack; the ambulance quickly got him to the hospital where his wife worked and he was saved. A few years later, after Twin Rivers closed in June 2018, Butch had another medical emergency; the trip to get care took much longer and he died before ever seeing a heart surgeon.

"How many more people have to die?" Cindy Anderson asked. "There are people dying in ambulances I think could have been saved." A physician at the hospital for 29 years, Dr. Dave Jain, told McGreal, "We're having probably three to five more deaths a month without having the hospital here."

The town's mayor, Dr. Chancellor Wayne, said that CHS closed the hospital "out of greed." He noted that while he could send his patients to a hospital across the border in Arkansas for an $800 MRI, CHS's fancy new hospital an hour up the highway charged $5,000.

Instead of putting the old hospital building up for sale or rent to anybody else who might have wanted to run a profitable rural hospital, the company paid the property taxes, cut the power, stripped the building, and let it rot for a full year. Twelve months, it turns out, is the exact amount of time a building would have to remain empty to force any new company that wanted to run it to spend "millions of dollars in renovations for it to reopen as a medical facility."

And the monopolists are on the move. Of the nation's roughly 2,000 rural hospitals, an estimated 673 are at risk of closure, according to the National Rural Health Association.

When I grew up in Lansing, Michigan, there were three hospitals in the area, all nonprofits. One had been endowed in 1912 by a cofounder of the Oldsmobile car company, the second run by the Catholic Church, and the third run by the county. Now all three are controlled or run by for-profit entities.

Prior to the Reagan era, hospitals and insurance companies were mostly run as nonprofits, the idea being that they should serve people and communities instead of shareholders. They were considered close cousins of the natural commons revered by our Founders.

Although Richard Nixon is blamed for the rise of for-profit health insurance and hospitals (he signed a law legalizing for-profit HMOs in 1973), both industries were already creeping in the for-profit direction.

As Reagan simultaneously ended antitrust enforcement and deregulated the finance industry, he all but assured the rise of hospital (and health insurance) monopolies. The sharks moved in, bought up or forced out of business the true nonprofits, and now largely control both fields.

Monopoly in Media: How Big Money Controls the Stories We Tell

Our liberty depends on the freedom of the press, and that cannot be limited without being lost.

–Thomas Jefferson in 1786, to his close friend Dr. James Currie

In 1983, 90% of the American media landscape (including magazines, books, music, news feeds, newspapers, movies, radio, and television) was dominated by 50 conglomerates.

Just 36 years later in 2019, a mere *five* conglomerates dominated 90% of the media that Americans consume (Time Warner, Disney, Murdoch's News Corporation, Bertelsmann of Germany, and Viacom).[15]

Looking at terrestrial radio in particular, the radio network that airs Rush Limbaugh and Sean Hannity—iHeartMedia—owns 850 radio stations in 150 markets across the country.[16]

After Reagan stopped enforcing the Sherman Antitrust Act and the Supreme Court started using Bork's strict interpretation of antitrust, there was an explosion of acquisitions and mergers in every sector of the economy. Thirteen years later, Bill Clinton signed the Telecommunications Act of 1996, which led to an even more startling concentration of media in a very few hands by eliminating rules about the maximum number of media outlets a family or company could own. As a result, freedom of the press in America today is as much an economic issue as a political one.

In 2003, after Louise and I sold our last business in Atlanta and retired to rural Vermont, we drove to Michigan to visit family for Thanksgiving. All the way there, we searched the radio dial for an intelligent conversation to listen to, but city after city all we found was Sean Hannity at a Habitat for Humanity site (he called it "Hannity for Humanity"), telling us that "no liberal" was ever going to live in the house they were helping build.

It was a bizarre experience. Having worked in radio back in the '60s and '70s, I had some knowledge of the industry, so when we got home from Michigan, I wrote an article, "Talking Back to Talk Radio," about how liberal talk radio might succeed, if done right. Sheldon and Anita Drobny, a pair of progressive venture capitalists, read my article online, and as Sheldon noted in his book *Road to Air America: Breaking the Right Wing Stranglehold on Our Nation's Airwaves* (in which he reprinted the article), it became the template for a business plan for that ultimately ill-fated network.

But rather than wait the almost two years it took the Drobnys to launch Air America, Louise and I, with the help of a local radio guy and friend, Rama Schneider, looked around Vermont and found a station in Burlington that was willing to put us on the air. The slot was Saturday mornings at 10 a.m., right after the swap-and-shop, so many of our callers, instead of discussing politics, wanted to know, "Is that John Deere still available?"

Ed Asner was kind enough to come on as a guest, helping us make a tape that caught the interest of the I.E. America Radio Network, run out of Detroit by the United Automobile Workers. Suddenly, broadcasting from our living room in Montpelier, Vermont, in a studio I'd thrown together for a few hundred dollars mostly from parts bought on eBay, we were on the air nationally, including Sirius satellite radio, taking on Rush Limbaugh (and beating him in some markets) in the noon-to-3-p.m. slot to this day.

In 2004, when Air America was finally rolled out, it was successful for as long as it was in large part because its programs were carried by stations owned by what was then Clear Channel and is now iHeartMedia: we were on more than 50 Clear Channel stations in the nation's major markets.

Following a string of Democratic victories in cities and states where Clear Channel was carrying Air America shows, the company was purchased in a leveraged buyout by Mitt Romney's Bain Capital and Thomas Lee.

Around that time, Clear Channel began pulling Air America's progressive programming off the air, dramatically cutting Air America's audience and their advertising revenue. The new progressive network was soon bankrupt, and two years later so was Clear Channel (because of the debt load dumped on it by Romney's business model), then reincarnated as iHeartMedia.

Meanwhile, the right-wing media machine continues to elect Republicans with big funding from right-wing corporations and the billionaires who own them and fund right-wing think tanks. As Ken Vogel et al. pointed out in a 2011 article for Politico, "The Heritage Foundation pays about $2 million [a year] to sponsor Limbaugh's show and about $1.3 million to do the same with Hannity's—and considers it money well spent."[17]

To the best of my knowledge, none of the talkers on the left have ever been funded in such a fashion. Small wonder that Hannity now owns a real estate empire worth tens of millions, and Limbaugh can brag of an eight-figure net worth or more.

But more important, the influence of those two well-financed talkers has altered America's political landscape in less than three decades. What this shows is that the movers and shakers on the far right, the libertarian billionaires, understand the power of media (and took Lewis Powell's advice).

Those of great wealth who are aligned with the left in America, however, have always largely ignored media, probably because they grew up in an America with the Fairness Doctrine and before the 1996 Telecommunications Act, and they always just assumed that "the truth will eventually be known."

But investing in political media can produce a huge return on investment and transform the politics of the nation. That's certainly what Roger Ailes and Rupert Murdoch thought when they lost an average of $90 million a year for about five years before the Fox News Channel became profitable.

The Early Days of Fox: Losing Money to Gain Political Power

Conservative commentator Brit Hume noted, in a 1999 interview with PBS, "This operation [Fox News] loses money. It doesn't lose nearly as much as it did at first, and it's—well, it's hit all its projections in terms of, you know, turning a profit, but it's—it will lose money now, and we expect for a couple more years. I think it's losing about $80 million to $90 million a year."

But that loss wasn't viewed by these right-wing billionaires as a "loss"—rather, it was an *investment*.

It's what Reverend Moon believed, as his *Washington Times* newspaper lost hundreds of millions of dollars but spread right-wing perspectives that influenced the nation. It's how the Koch brothers have referred to the hundreds of millions they shower on right-wing politicians and causes. And it's what the people who started Air America Radio believed, although they couldn't get big funders to understand the stakes.

While Rupert Murdoch lost hundreds of millions of dollars (Air America's bankruptcy was for $14 million) in its first few years, Murdoch hung on and kept pouring in the cash. And it put George W. Bush in the White House, according to several independent analyses.

As Richard Morin wrote for the *Washington Post* in 2006, asking rhetorically, "Does President Bush owe his controversial win in 2000 to Fox cable television news?"[18] The answer was an emphatic "Yes!" according to academics who did exhaustive research into what they called "the Fox Effect."

As Morin reported:

> *"Our estimates imply that Fox News convinced 3 to 8 percent of its audience to shift its voting behavior towards the Republican Party, a sizable media persuasion effect," said Stefano DellaVigna of the University of California at Berkely [sic] and Ethan Kaplan of Stockholm University.*
>
> *In Florida alone, they estimate, the Fox Effect may have produced more than 10,000 additional votes for Bush— clearly a decisive factor in a state he carried by fewer than 600 votes.*

The analysis looked at the vote from 1996 to 2004 in 9,256 American cities and towns where Fox was available on basic cable. "They found," reported Morin, "clear evidence of a Fox

Effect among non-Republicans in the presidential and Senate races, even after controlling for other factors including vote trends in similar nearby towns without access to Fox." The researchers added that "the Fox effect seems to [be] permanent and may be increasing." And that was in 2006.

This is problematic, because no democracy can survive intact when only one voice or political perspective overwhelmingly dominates any major branch of the media.

Literally hundreds of right-wing talk show hosts, both local and national, are broadcasting every day, all day, in every town and city in America.

Progressive voices, on the other hand, are few and far between; in most parts of America (and virtually all of rural America), the only radio signal that carries any progressive programming whatsoever is SiriusXM, which requires a subscription and special receiver—costs that are hard to bear among voters in the reddest states where Republican policies have destroyed unions and exported jobs overseas, thus leading to widespread poverty.

Jefferson made his comment about newspapers being vital to America just at the time he was being most viciously attacked in the newspapers. The core requisite of democracy is debate. When there's only a single predominant voice in the media, American democracy itself is at greatest risk, be that voice on the right or the left.

It's time to enforce antitrust in our media landscape and to bring back media ownership rules that both limit the number of outlets and prioritize local ownership.

Unbundling Cable, Phones, and TV

Unbundling is the word that the multibillion-dollar industry that controls much of our news and politics, our understanding of the world and our interactions with each other, doesn't want us to discuss. But it may well be one of the most vital words for all Americans to understand. And it's at the core of effective challenges to monopoly, particularly with regard to tech.

Unbundling could cut your TV, phone, and internet bills from an average of around $180 collectively to around $30 or $40 a month. It would diminish the control that giant ISP corporations like Comcast and AT&T have over our ability to access information. And it would create space for competition in the telecommunications sector generally and providers of internet access particularly.

Bundling is one of the most powerful ways some of the largest and most consequential companies in America maintain their wealth and power. They maintain—and grow—their wealth in the old-fashioned way that monopolists always do—price gouging and crushing competitors. They maintain—and grow—their power over both citizens and government by deploying their money and their influencing power over media (from cable TV to the internet).

The "bundle" at the core of this is the connection between the "pipe" (the wire, cable, fiber, or 5G ability to deliver internet and cable TV service to you) and the internet, phone, and TV content itself.

There are two parts here, which in America are bundled but in much of the rest of the world are unbundled. They were unbundled here in the United States, at least with regard to the internet, as recently as the 1990s.

The two parts are the pipes and what goes through them.

When it comes to digital data—unlike water, where there's typically only a single source—there are tens of thousands of companies around the world that provide internet flow and data to companies and consumers. In countries that have successfully unbundled their internet pipes from the data, these companies compete with each other on the basis of cost, features, and services to provide people with their internet access. The main result of that competition is lower prices for consumers.

This is why bundled internet, TV, and phone service that typically costs around $180 a month in the United States (where we bundle pipes and data) costs typically around $30 in France for the same (and often even better) service.

Since FCC Chairman and former Verizon lawyer Ajit Pai killed net neutrality in 2017, American internet service providers are now doing what Google, Facebook, and other companies have practiced: detailed monitoring of your online activity and then using and/or selling that information.

The difference between Google and Comcast (for example) is that you can choose not to use Google, or even use one of their competitors like DuckDuckGo, which explicitly does not gather, track, or record users' information. But if Comcast is the only company with a fiber or cable coming into your house, you simply do not have the ability (short of jumping through elaborate tech hoops like getting a virtual private network, or VPN) to prevent them from seeing every website you visit, reading every username and password you enter anywhere, and consolidating and selling that information without informing you.

However, when the data going through the pipe and the pipe itself are unbundled, so that Comcast may still own and maintain the pipe into your house but you choose to get your internet services through another internet service provider (ISP) altogether, those ISP companies can connect to you through invisible and maintenance-free VPN-like protocols, and Comcast loses access to your personal information. (It would also be possible for Congress or the FCC to categorize the company that owns the pipe coming into your home as a *common carrier*, meaning that by law they can't snoop on you. The Obama administration did this, but it was reversed by Trump and Pai.)

Phone companies have been regulated as common carriers since the early 20th century. This means that they must respect your privacy (just as the post office can't open and read your mail without due process). It also means that they can't base pricing or other decisions on what you're discussing or with whom you're discussing it (outside of long-distance charges).

Your phone company can't listen in on your call and then send you a bill that says, "Because you were discussing business with your boss, we're charging you an extra $.10 a minute." Or, "Because you were discussing your cancer diagnosis with your doctor, you'll be getting material in the mail from a hospital that offers excellent cancer care."

On the other hand, your ISP can do this. They don't yet do it as explicitly as those examples, but it already happens in a big way in the commercial sphere.

For example, when my wife was diagnosed with breast cancer a decade ago, even though she never mentioned it in any public place (or even in a private forum), she started getting ads for breast cancer therapies, breast prostheses, and chemo wigs on pretty much any computer she used when visiting ad-supported websites.

Even the big email providers are now reading every word you send and receive (so they can "improve your user experience"); it may simply be that Louise's correspondence with her doctor or a few close relatives got sold into the breast cancer industry marketplace.

On the "who you're talking to" front, ISPs now have the ability to (and are already engaging in the practice, some suggest) speed up sites that pay them or slow down the loading of sites either that don't pay them or with whose politics they disagree (sites advocating net neutrality or unbundling, for example).

Turning Financial Power into Political Power

Fox News isn't the only example of a business that is willing to cut into its profits for the short term in order to change minds and drum up support for policies that will make it richer in the long run.

Just prior to the 2016 presidential election, the Progressive Change Institute commissioned a nationwide poll conducted by the highly respected firm GBAO Strategies. The result showed clearly just how deep and extensive is the problem of monopolistic, legalized political bribery in America.[19]

When asked whether the US government should negotiate prescription drug prices, 79% of Americans agreed and only 12% opposed. But because Big Pharma bribed Congress to the tune of $2.5 billion over the last decade, giving money to 9 out of 10 members of the House and 97 out of 100 members of the Senate, nothing has changed.[20] Tens of thousands of Americans die every year because of this bribery.[21]

Seventy-one percent of Americans (including 56% of Republicans) say that *all* Americans should have access to a debt-free college education, but banks spent millions bribing DC politicians to keep George W. Bush's Bankruptcy Abuse Prevention and Consumer Protection Act of 2005 in place so that students can't discharge student loan debt in bankruptcy.[22] At the same time, colleges and universities spent additional millions bribing politicians to ignore the soaring costs of higher education: as the *Wall Street Journal* reported in 2015, colleges and universities have become one of the most effective lobbying forces in Washington, "employing more lobbyists last year than any other industries except drug manufacturing and technology."[23]

A 2015 survey of likely 2016 voters found that fully 71% of Americans (and 63% of Republicans) supported giving "all Americans the choice of buying health insurance through Medicare or private insurers," but the massively profitable health insurance industry spent over $158 million in 2018 bribing and influencing politicians to maintain their *billions* in quarterly profits.[24]

The list of issues and industries where bribery has corrupted our legislative system could easily fill a book of its own.

Issues blocked politically by special interest groups and billionaires include the following: infrastructure jobs program (71% support, with 55% of Republicans); expanding Social Security benefits (70% support, 62% GOP voters); getting corporate executives out of "revolving door" government positions (59% support, 55% GOP); guaranteeing net neutrality (61% support, with 52% of Republicans); breaking up big banks (71% of Democrats and 51% of GOP); restoring the top 50% income tax rate that Reagan nuked (71% Democratic support, 53% GOP); and reprising FDR's "government as the employer of last resort" job programs to rebuild America (83% Democratic support, 55% GOP).[25]

About 70% of Americans are concerned about climate change, but we're not holding the fossil fuel industry accountable.[26] Oil Change International documented in their study of the impact of oil industry lobbying, "In the 2015–2016 election cycle oil, gas and coal companies spent $354 million in campaign contributions and lobbying and received $29.4 billion in federal subsidies over those same years—an 8,200% return on investment."[27]

Americans are dying from vaping, but there's still no regulation of "inhalable" drugs like nicotine because of decades of aggressive bribery of politicians by the tobacco industry.[28]

We're watching the destruction of public education by for-profit charter schools,[29] while the private prison industry is lobbying for more free prison labor and more kids in cages.[30]

Businesses, because of deregulation from Reagan to Trump, are pumping more poison in our air, water, and food[31] and exploiting low-income workers and people in the military via payday lenders.[32]

Meanwhile, we helplessly watch an orgy of gun violence in the United States[33] as our country spends more on our military than the next eight countries combined.[34]

It all goes back to one thing: bribery by monopolistic interests.

Political bribery has always been a problem, but it exploded during the Reagan administration because in 1976 the US Supreme Court had said,[35] for the first time in American history, that when billionaires and corporations bribed legislators, it was a matter of First Amendment–protected free speech; the Court later amplified that with its corrupt 2010 *Citizens United* decision.[36]

Because of this, today the odds of legislation that puts the interests of working people first is equivalent to random chance, as Princeton's Gilens and Page found in a massive 2014 study.[37]

Martin Gilens wrote in the *Boston Review* in 2012, "When preferences diverge, the views of the affluent make a big difference, while support among the middle class and the poor has almost no relationship to policy outcomes. . . . [T]he support or opposition of the poor or the middle class has no impact on a policy's prospects of being adopted."[38]

At the September 12, 2019, Democratic debate there wasn't a single question about the bribery of our legislators by billionaires and corporations; only Bernie Sanders and Elizabeth Warren pointed out the "corruption" problem, and their comments were ignored by all the other candidates—who were competing with each other and the GOP for billionaire and corporate money.[39]

There are movements to get money out of politics (such as Move to Amend,[40] among others), but the flow of money into our politics has dampened any serious discussion from our corporate media and bought-off political leaders.

So long as corporations are considered "persons" that can spend unlimited amounts of money in our politics, the monopolists will continue to flood our legislatures with corrupting money.

The Racial Wealth Monopoly

That is not a just government, nor is property secure under it, where arbitrary restrictions, exemptions, and monopolies deny to part of its citizens that free use of their faculties, and free choice of their occupations, which not only constitute their property in the general sense of the word; but are their means of acquiring property strictly so called.

–James Madison, Property, March 29, 1792[41]

While the monopolization of wealth and political power by giant corporations and the billionaires they create has reached crisis proportions in this country, the monopolization of middle-class wealth by white people—and, particularly, white men—is also a crisis that keeps our country unequal and out of balance.

My mother's family came to this country in the late 1600s from Wales and settled in Massachusetts. They did well over the generations; there are still places in that state named after the family, and since the early 1700s it's a safe bet (looking at genealogical records my mom painstakingly compiled for decades) they were literate and educated. So it was only natural that Mom would go to college and graduate magna cum laude; her family was white.

My dad's parents came to America from Grimstad, Norway, in 1917 and settled first in Chicago and then in northern Michigan. They were literate and educated, and by the 1930s they owned their own home in northern Michigan. My dad went to college for a few years on the GI Bill before dropping out because Mom got pregnant with me; he later bought a home with a loan made possible by the GI Bill. His family was white.

By the time I came along, my parents had benefited from centuries of education and wealth-building directed almost exclusively to white people. That's not to say we were wealthy; my mom's family lost everything in the Great Depression, and, in part because of that, her father died of a heart attack in his 30s when she was 13 years old. My grandmother raised her alone, working as the town clerk in Charlevoix, Michigan.

My dad's father was a craftsman—a cabinetmaker—and made fine furniture, including, according to family lore, a piece that's in the White House. But Dad only inherited from them his education and outlook: until I was five or six years old, he made a living selling Rexair vacuum cleaners and World Book Encyclopedias door-to-door, and we lived in a tiny two-room house in the poor part of downtown Lansing before he got a good union job in a tool-and-die shop that catapulted us into the suburban middle class.

I tell this history to illustrate that it's a fairly common one for white Americans. Those of us descended from Europeans have almost always had at least a baseline of literacy and the generation-to-generation transmission of a sort of cultural wealth going back centuries that gave us an edge over African Americans and nonwhite Hispanics.

We also benefited from centuries of laws and policies in this nation that nakedly favored white people, even long after the end of both slavery *and* Jim Crow. My dad could go to college on the GI Bill and buy a house with its help, but of the first 67,000 mortgages that the GI Bill made possible, as Jamiles Lartey wrote for the *Guardian*, "fewer than 100 were taken out by non-white people."[42]

This is particularly critical because home equity represents the vast majority of wealth held by middle-class and working-class families in America.

The house Dad bought when I was six for $13,000 in south Lansing was in an all-white neighborhood; most of the other dads in the neighborhood were also World War II vets like him and probably bought their houses the same way he did. And even if an African American family had succeeded in buying a home in our lower-middle-class neighborhood, they may not have lasted long before being harassed out of their new house.

I went to a brand-new school (the entire subdivision, including the school, was built in 1957, the year we moved in, on what had previously been cornfields) and got a first-rate education. An education system funded largely by property taxes did, in the 1950s and today, what it was designed to do in the late 1800s and early 1900s as public schools spread across the country: keep prosperous neighborhoods prosperous for future generations through good education, while letting poorer neighborhoods—particularly those where black people lived—basically rot.

While Democratic Keynesian economics put into place by FDR in the 1930s created the middle class intentionally, it was also intentionally a *white* middle class, with numerous guardrails to keep it that way. The institutional barriers to people of color building wealth through education or home ownership did not vanish with the Civil Rights Act in the 1960s; as recently as 2012, Wells Fargo pleaded guilty to pushing black and Hispanic families into exploding subprime mortgages while steering white families into traditional fixed-rate 30-year mortgages.

During the era from the 1930s to the 1980s, FDR's New Deal economic policies of unionization and high progressive taxes kept wealth inequality at bay; the middle class actually grew their wealth and income faster than the top 1% did. And when the '60s and '70s came along and many of the entry barriers that blacks and Hispanics had previously faced began to fall (particularly in government hiring, which is nearly 20% of the economy), the middle class began to grow beyond just white people.

Chicago School libertarian trickle-down Reaganomics (particularly his war on unions and his tax cuts for corporations and the ultrarich) put an end to all that: they halted the growth of wealth and income for working people and erased the gains of minority families who were just beginning to emerge into the middle class but didn't yet have multigenerational education or wealth to fall back on.

The wealth monopoly in America isn't just the concentration of money in the hands of the top 1%; it's also the concentration of wealth among white people.

Those Reaganomics policies that America has been groaning under since 1981—even through two Democratic presidential administrations—continue to push people of color underwater. Referencing a 2017 study by the Economic Policy Institute, a headline in the *Guardian* summarizes the entire crisis in a single sentence: "Median wealth of black Americans 'will fall to zero by 2053' warns new report."[43]

It's not just white people who have seized almost all working- and middle-class wealth; it's largely white *men*. While black men faced huge barriers to education, housing, and good jobs up to and through the 1970s (and still do, albeit less explicitly), so did white women (albeit less severe).

Prior to the early 1970s, women couldn't get a credit card without their husband's signature, pretty much regardless of their wealth or income.[44] Women weren't allowed to serve on a jury in most states until the mid-1970s,[45] and possession of birth control—even for married women—was illegal in some states until 1965, when the US Supreme Court, in *Griswold v. Connecticut*, struck down that state's law criminalizing the possession of condoms, diaphragms, and birth control pills even for married couples in their own homes.[46]

Women had a separate area in the help wanted section of the newspaper, and getting pregnant (or even married, for jobs like flight attendant or waitress) was a firing offense. Ivy League and military colleges were almost entirely all male until the 1970s (not to mention all white), and in 1963, white working women earned 59 cents for every dollar earned by white men (the ratios were similar across races).[47]

Much good work was done by civil rights and women's rights legislation in the 1960s and 1970s, but conservative white men have continued to block the Equal Rights Amendment, which simply says, "Equality of rights under the law shall not be denied or abridged by the United States or by any state on account of sex," since it was first written by Alice Paul and introduced to Congress in 1923. "Conservative" men have blocked it every year for generations.

While the top 1% now owns more wealth than the entire bottom 90%, the 61% of America that is made up of non-Hispanic white people[48] owns the majority of middle-class wealth: for every $100 in wealth held by white families, black families have $5.04.[49] It's hard to find a clear gender breakout of that white wealth, but it's safe to say the majority of it is held by the roughly 30% of Americans who are white men.

These racial and gender-based monopolies of wealth in America keep down women and nonwhites, while producing a significant drag on the economic and cultural vitality of our nation.

Monopolies over Labor

When people consider monopolies, or even highly concentrated markets like airlines or pharmaceuticals, generally the only thing they think of is the ability of companies in concentrated markets to set prices wherever they'd like. But there are fully three primary benefits to monopoly or oligopoly, from the monopolists' point of view.

In addition to *setting prices* by restricting competition, monopolies can (and typically do) *drive down wages* so that they end up with a steady supply of cheap labor, and—both by market (selling) control and labor market (workers) control—they send vastly *more money flowing to stockholders and senior management* than can companies in truly competitive marketplaces.

Cheap Labor, and Getting Cheaper

At its core, virtually every aspect of the movement that embraced monopoly (Bork actually wrote about all the "lost" inventions, innovations, and profits that were caused by a lack of monopoly!) boiled down to cheap labor. Joe Lyles, writing as Conceptual Guerilla, put up a brilliant analysis of this more than a decade ago titled "Defeat the Right in Three Minutes," suggesting that quite literally everything we call "conservative" was really about driving down wages. While racial hatred and misogyny also play big roles these days in the "conservative" movement, there's still a lot of truth to Lyles's analysis.[50]

- Cheap-labor conservatives don't want a national health care system, because they want workers to be dependent on their employers and thus willing to accept lower wages.

- Cheap-labor conservatives hate the minimum wage and unions because both support wage floors and, over time, raise wages for working people.

- Cheap-labor conservatives want women relatively powerless (particularly over their own reproductive functions) so that, as in the era before the 1970s, they'll work for far less than today's $.78 to a man's dollar.

- Cheap-labor conservatives go on and on about, as Lyles notes, "morality, virtue, respect for authority, hard work and other 'values'" so that when workers can't climb the ladder, society will blame it on the individuals instead of a system rigged to maintain cheap labor.

- Cheap-labor conservatives encourage bigotry, fear, and hatred to prevent working people from seeing their commonality of human and economic interests, regardless of race, gender identity, or the urban/rural divide.

America has a long history with the cheap-labor crowd: slavery was the ultimate expression of this "conservative" value system, and under the 13th Amendment, it continues to be legally practiced in the United States in our for-profit prison systems.

The 13th Amendment didn't actually end slavery in the United States; it merely turned it over to prisons, be they state-run or for-profit corporations. It reads: "Neither slavery nor involuntary servitude, except as a punishment for crime whereof the party shall have been duly convicted, shall exist within the United States." As a result, the pressure on Congress and state legislatures from for-profit prison corporations to increase criminal penalties to give them more *literal* slave labor has exploded.

Cheap-labor conservatives, it turns out, are also huge fans of monopoly and oligopoly, in large part because these systems keep wages low. There's a marketplace for labor, just like for everything else, and when a small number of corporations control a large number of employment venues, they can simply keep wages low through that market power. Check out the pay of fast-food workers or flight attendants or nurses back in the 1960s compared with today; every industry that concentrates or consolidates sees wages go down.

Less for Labor Means More for CEOs

Monopoly also produces extremes of inequality, and extreme inequality kills societies.

Richard Wilkinson and Kate Pickett of the Equality Trust in the UK have done extensive research on the topic, leading to two best-selling books and a brilliant website.[51] They document in startling detail, going nation by nation and, in the United States, state by state, how inequality damages the lives of everybody except those who live in massive wealth bubbles at the top.

It's not the poverty that extreme inequality produces that does much of the damage. Instead, because we're wired like all mammals to understand and perceive both fairness and unfairness, when we find ourselves in unfair situations, our interactions with the world and each other become distorted. (These experiments have also been done with dogs and monkeys,[52] among others; every mammal studied reacts negatively to inequality and unfairness.)

Wilkinson and Pickett have documented how, as society becomes progressively less fair and more unequal, a whole host of cultural and psychological problems ripple across the culture. These are *not* caused by poverty, but simply by *inequality*, and include the following:

- Less social cohesion and trust among people
- More teenage pregnancies and STDs
- More crime, from shoplifting to murder to mass shootings
- Decreased worker productivity
- Increased suicide
- Lower grades in school
- Increased mortality and morbidity, shorter life spans
- Increased obesity and the diseases associated with it
- Higher levels of mental illness, including diseases thought to be totally "organic," like schizophrenia
- Lower rates of social and political engagement
- Less empathy and altruism among and between individuals (making for a more brutal society)

But inequality isn't just driven by tax cuts or hoarding by rich people. Instead, in country after country, state after state, the main driver of inequality is market concentration, also known as monopoly and oligopoly. The tax cuts and hoarding are the result of the political and economic power this market concentration brings.

Lina Khan and Sandeep Vaheesan produced a brilliant scientific analysis of this phenomenon published in the *Harvard Law and Policy Review*,[53] and followed it up with a more consumer-friendly analysis in the *Washington Post*.[54]

Simply using monopoly labor market power, for example, senior executives at Google, Apple, Intel, Intuit, Pixar, and

Adobe had "stolen" an estimated $3 billion from 60,000 workers when the illegal collusion between the companies was uncovered by the Justice Department in 2010.

They reported on how 20,000 nurses in Detroit lost an estimated $400 million between 2002 and 2006 because of hospital consolidation and collusion among hospitals in hiring.

While these examples represent actual crimes against persons by these giant corporations, trillions of dollars have been upwardly redistributed from working people to the top 1% over the past four decades by corporate giants in ways that are generally less visible and perfectly legal but wouldn't work without high levels of market concentration.

Much of it is because the political and economic power that comes with massive corporate oligopolies allows CEOs and senior executives to take pretty much whatever paycheck they want. As the Economic Policy Institute notes, "From 1978 to 2018, CEO compensation grew by 1,007.5%, far outstripping S&P stock market growth (706.7%) and the wage growth of very high earners (339.2%). In contrast, wages for the typical worker grew by just 11.9%."[55]

In the preceding 40 years, prior to Reagan's introduction of trickle-down neoliberalism, working people actually saw their wages grow at a *higher rate* than the CEO class (although CEOs were doing just fine, thank you very much). But Reagan's cutting the top income tax rate from 74% to 28% gave CEOs carte blanche to take as much as they could.

As the *Wall Street Journal* revealed in 2007, William "Dollar Bill" McGuire, the CEO of insurance giant UnitedHealth, took over a billion dollars in compensation.[56] One could argue that much of it came from the company telling people, "No, we're not going to pay your claim; we just discovered you had a preexisting condition (or you hit your lifetime limit)." His successor, Stephen J. Hemsley, walked away with hundreds of millions.[57]

America used to have a thriving middle class; in 2019, fully 40% of Americans struggled to pay for food, housing, utilities, or medical care.[58] Half of adult Americans have *no* retirement savings, and nearly two-thirds would be wiped out financially with an unexpected expense like a medical bill or accident costing only $500.[59]

Meanwhile, even entrepreneurs are being wiped out. Khan and Vaheesan document how creation of new businesses in America dropped by 53% between 1977 and 2010.

What has changed so much in America in the past 40 years? Simple. Reagan and the Supreme Court put Robert Bork's theories into effect, and our formerly diverse and competitive corporate landscape has been wiped out, replaced by a few hundred giant corporations that control nearly every aspect of our economy—and our politics.

Solution: Democracy's Immune System

If the continuous accumulation of wealth and the political power associated with it is a cancer in our economic, political, and social system, then the immune system that can take it on is an empowered middle class.

A middle class that outnumbers both the rich and poor combined is a uniquely American invention. At our nation's founding, the middle class made up the majority of free

Americans, in part because land stolen from the Indians was so cheap, and free slave labor helped produce a general prosperity for white people.

While the source of the American middle class in the 18th century may have been pernicious, the lesson for us today is how it produced a general economic, political, and social stability. Fully two-thirds of white people in America at the time of the American Revolution owned land and thus were largely self-sufficient. Meanwhile, in England only a fifth of the population owned land or had any control over their own economic destiny. The middle class of that era was a very small group of shopkeepers, doctors, lawyers, and small businessmen (like Charles Dickens's Ebenezer Scrooge, who had a one-office company with a single employee).

Wealth and land were highly concentrated in the England of 1776, as was the political power that flowed from that wealth. To keep the middle class from expanding, England even had "maximum wage" laws, punishing employers who paid workers too much. The rest of Europe was in a similar situation, a remnant of feudal times.

In America in 1776, the top 1% of Americans received only around 8.5% of the income, with the rest of it widely distributed among working people. Today, the top 1% get around 20% of all income, leaving far less for the rest. This has gutted today's middle class. While almost two-thirds of Americans were middle class in the decade before Reaganomics, today it's slipped below the 50% danger-mark threshold.

The loss of economic power by America's working people has paralleled a loss of political power. Prior to Reaganomics, labor unions effectively balanced the economic and political power of big business and its lobbyists, so much so that a mere $200 million was spent on lobbying per year in the first years of Reagan's administration. Today, with Reaganomics firmly entrenched and labor unions decimated, corporate and billionaire spending on lobbying runs well over $3 billion a year.

This rupturing of working Americans' economic and political power has not just produced anxiety and despair; it's also caused Americans to disengage from politics because they rightly view the political system as hopelessly corrupt and only beholden to the billionaires and the corporations that made them rich.

Solution: Replace the "Consumer Welfare" Framework

Robert Bork's consumer welfare framework for determining if a company is a monopoly concerns itself with only two outcomes:

1. Low prices for consumers
2. High returns for investors

But if a company is concerned only with consumers and investors, then it is going to squeeze everything else, from environmental protection to wages and worker safety to product quality. This is also an incentive to cut labor expenses by merging with other companies and eliminating entire departments. The new company won't need two sales, HR, or accounting departments; tens of thousands of jobs are typically lost in large mergers.

Bork's policy, now America's policy, means that companies now cut pensions as a way of cutting liabilities. It means that all firms are encouraged to cut corners on environmental, workplace, and consumer protections, and to lobby endlessly to kill those protections entirely.

Corporate stakeholders should include workers and their unions, who arguably have the greatest interest in maintaining the solvency of a corporation, because their wages depend on it.

An extension of the workers and their families' stake in locally owned nonmonopolistic companies are communities as a whole. We've seen across America's Rust Belt, where once-thriving towns and cities have been mired in deepening despair since the 1980s as a result of neoliberal trade policies, the fruits of trickle-down Reaganomics, and the adoption of Bork's consumer welfare framework.

In some industries, such as heavy manufacturing and chemical processing, the impact on the environment is clear and immediate in the form of pollution discharged into the air and waterways. But every corporation has an environmental footprint.

Cloud-based companies are dependent on stable power production, which means that massive servers like Amazon Web Services can have equally massive carbon footprints. With more and more goods being shipped across the United States, the wear and tear on our nation's roads not only is a concern for infrastructure but also means increasing environmental costs associated with asphalt and tire debris in the air and runoff directly from the roads, along with salts and de-icers in the winter—all costs that are dumped onto the public and the commons.

Finally, there is the corporation itself. A corporation can be a positive institution in a community—a touchstone for workers and families to gain dignity for their work, and for the community to take pride in the manufacture of goods that are distributed across the country.

That sense was lost to Bork's doctrine as corporate raiders and vulture capitalists like Carl Icahn and Mitt Romney began to gobble up corporations and strip their assets (this is the crux of the plot of Oliver Stone's *Wall Street*).

All of these stakeholders (workers, families, communities, the environment, competing corporations, governments, and the corporations themselves) can either benefit or be hurt by a large corporation's actions. All are ignored by Bork's doctrine.

The solution is to reverse Bork's community-killing consumer welfare framework and return to real antitrust regulation, like what we had in part from Senator John Sherman's time until the Supreme Court and Reagan put Bork's bizarre theory into practice.

Solution: Break Up the Internet Giants

I was oblivious to the real significance of Facebook in everyday life until the company disabled my personal, private account. The list of possible reasons they posted for doing this included "impersonating a celebrity," so maybe they shut me down because they thought I was pretending to be that guy who's a talk show host and author (ahem).

It's also possible that somebody at Facebook took offense to my interviewing Judd Legum[60] around that time about the groundbreaking research he's been publishing over at popular

.info pointing out the right-wing, pro-Trump slant that Facebook's corporate management and founder took in 2019.[61] Fact is, though, I have no idea why they did it, although my account spontaneously reappeared a few weeks after an earlier version of this chapter appeared as an article on Salon.com and other sites.

When they first disabled my account and asked me to upload my driver's license (which I did at least seven times over several weeks), I figured it was a mistake. Then, a month or two later, they delivered the final verdict: I was out. I could download all my information if I wanted before they finally closed the door, but even when I tried to create a new account using my personal email address, they blocked my attempt, saying that I already had a (disabled) account and thus couldn't create another.

I checked Facebook only once a week on average, and only followed close friends and my widely scattered relatives, having configured my personal account to be as private as possible. I figured I could do without knowing what my cousins' kids, or my nieces and nephews, were up to; I could just call them or send them Christmas cards, after all. And the Salem International private group of international relief workers I was a member of could keep me up to date through our email listserv.[62]

What I discovered in the weeks after I was dumped by Facebook, particularly when one of my Salem friends in Germany was badly injured in a car accident, was that I was shockingly reliant on Facebook to keep in touch with family and friends. As the Joni Mitchell song goes, you don't know what you've got till it's gone.

Which raises the question, has Facebook gone from being merely a destination on the internet to being so interwoven in our lives that it should now be considered part of the commons and regulated as such?

Is it time to discuss taking Facebook out of private, for-profit hands?

Or, alternatively, is it time for the federal government to break up Facebook or even create a national town square, an everyperson's civic center, to compete with it?

The history of Europe and the United States, particularly throughout the 19th century, often tells the story of how wealthy and powerful men would congregate in exclusive members-only men's clubs to determine the fate and future of governments, businesses, and even local communities.[63] You'll find them woven into much of the literature of that era, from Dickens to Doyle to Poe.

Because these clubs had strict membership requirements, they were often at the core of governmental and business power systems, helping maintain wealthy white male domination of society. The rules for both initial and continuing membership were typically developed and maintained by majority or even consensus agreement of their members, although the homogeneity of that membership pretty much ensured that women, men of color, and men of lower social or economic status never had a say in public or private institutional governance.

Then, at the cusp of the 20th century, things changed.

The first decade and a half of the 20th century saw an explosion of progressive reforms, best remembered as the time when progressive Republican presidents Theodore Roosevelt and William Howard Taft (who followed him) engaged in massive trust-busting, breaking up America's biggest monopolies to make room for local, small, and medium-sized businesses to grow.[64]

An often-overlooked phenomenon during that era was the creation of egalitarian, public civic centers across the country, usually built and owned by local or regional governments. While to this day men's clubs remain places where the brokers of great power and wealth can congregate, these new publicly owned civic centers replaced the much smaller and less comfortable public parks and private pubs as places where average citizens could socialize, strategize, and form political movements at no cost.

Progressive political movements like the suffragists used these public squares heavily, and they became an essential building block of movement politics (along with public schools—many states passed laws authorizing their auditoriums to be used as civic centers).[65]

Public dialogues and even local or regional discussions about local and national politics have moved from the men's clubs (1700–1900) to the civic centers (1901–1990s). Today they are held on the internet, another public space that was created by the US government (DARPA) and universities.

Facebook, however, figured out a way to privatize a large part of that public space and turn it into cash, making Mark Zuckerberg, at $77.8 billion, the eighth-richest person in the world.[66]

While Facebook was, in 2019 and 2020, embroiled in a controversy over whether it was wrong for it to allow Trump's political advertising that contained naked lies, the debate over fully or partially nationalizing the platform, or breaking up the company, has gotten much less coverage.

But it's an important issue and deserves more attention. Facebook was so critical to Donald Trump's 2016 election efforts, for example, that his 2016 digital media/Facebook manager, Brad Parscale, was elevated to managing the entire Trump 2020 effort—again, with Facebook at the center of it.

Political change flows out of public dialogue.

The American Revolution would probably never have gotten off the ground were it not for meeting places available to the public—the most famous being Sam Adams's tavern.[67] Similarly, churches open to the public (although privately owned but regulated on a nonprofit basis) were the core of the 20th century's civil rights movement.

Facebook has, for millions, replaced these public places as a nexus for social, cultural, and political interaction. As such, it resembles a part of the natural commons.

When radio achieved the equivalent of four hours of "screen time" a day for the average American, in 1927 and 1934 we passed comprehensive regulation of the industry to prevent the spread of disinformation and mandate responsible broadcasting practices.[68]

Similarly, our nation's telephone systems have been both nationalized (during World War I) and repeatedly heavily regulated since 1913 to ensure users' privacy and prevent the exploitation of customers or their personal information by Ma Bell.

For many Americans, Facebook is a primary source of news as well as a social, political, and civic activity center. It controls about a third of all web traffic.[69] Starting from scratch, it would be hard to imagine such a central nexus for these kinds of critical interactions without envisioning it as a natural commons, like a civic center or broadcasting service.

The company controls that commons in ways that invade Americans' privacy and disrupt democracy. Facebook's exploitation of user information has been so egregious that Senator Ron Wyden, D-Ore., one of America's most outspoken digital privacy advocates, has openly speculated about sending Mark Zuckerberg to prison.[70] As Wyden and others point out, we regulate radio, TV, and newspaper advertising; how did Facebook get a free pass when it has a larger "news" reach than any other medium?

One solution is to regulate Facebook like a public utility. Alternatively, the federal government could take majority ownership of the company—or fund an alternative to it—so that it or the government version of it could be run not just to enrich executives and stockholders but also, like the Ma Bell of old, to serve the public good.[71]

The dominance of Google in everything from email to internet search raises similar concerns. At least in the days of Ma Bell, I had access to a phone regardless of my politics or what I said on the phone, and the company couldn't sell access to the contents of my phone calls or a list of the people I called.

Solution: Bring Back
the Corporate Death Penalty

While the human death penalty has largely disappeared in the world and is fading in the United States (a good thing), the *corporate* death penalty needs a revival.

The corporate death penalty, widespread in the 19th century, is a political and economic process that weeds bad actors out of the business ecosystem to make room for good players. The process of revoking corporate charters goes back to the very first years of the United States. After all, the only reasons that states allow ("charter") corporations (normal business corporations can be chartered *only* by a state, not the federal government) are to serve the public interest.

As the Wyoming Constitution of 1889 laid out:

> *All powers and franchises of corporations are derived from the people and are granted by their agent, the government, for the public good and general welfare, and the right and duty of the state to control and regulate them for these purposes is hereby declared. The power, rights and privileges of any and all corporations may be forfeited by willful neglect or abuse thereof. The police power of the state is supreme over all corporations as well as individuals.*[72]

When a corporation does business ethically and legally, it serves its local community, its employees, its customers, *and* its shareholders. For over a century, American corporations were held to this very reasonable standard.

Beginning in 1784, Pennsylvania demanded that corporations include a revocation clause in corporate charters that automatically dissolved them after a few decades so they couldn't grow so large or so rich as to become a public menace. It also authorized the state to dissolve any corporation that harmed the state or its citizens, including harms to customers and employees. "Nor shall any charter for the purposes aforesaid be granted for a longer time than twenty years," Pennsylvania's corporate law read, "and every such charter shall contain a clause reserving to the legislature the power to alter, revoke, or annul the same, whenever in their opinion it may be injurious to the citizens of the commonwealth" (Article I, Section 25).[73]

As the United States grew, the federal government passed laws requiring corporate-death-penalty revocation clauses in the state corporate charters of insurance companies in 1809 and banks in 1814. By the late 1880s, every state required them for *all* business corporations.

From the founding of America to today, governments routinely revoked corporate charters, forcing liquidation and sale of assets, although it's been over a century since such efforts have focused on corporations large enough to have amassed financial and, thus, political power.

In the 19th century, banks were shut down for behaving in a "financially unsound" way in Ohio, Mississippi, and Pennsylvania. And when corporations that ran turnpikes in New York and Massachusetts didn't keep their roads in repair, those states gave the corporations the death sentence.

In 1825, Pennsylvania passed laws making it even easier for that state to "revoke, alter, or annul" corporate charters "whenever in their opinion [the operation of the corporation] may be injurious to citizens of the community," and by the 1870s, 19 states had gone through the long and tedious process of amending their state constitutions expressly to give legislators the power to terminate the existence of badly behaving corporations that originated or operated in those states.

Candidates have even run for public office (for example, Senator Elizabeth Warren in the 2020 Democratic presidential primary) and done very well or won on platforms including the revocation of corporate charters. One of the largest issues of the election of 1832 was Andrew Jackson's demand that the corporate charter of the Second Bank of the United States not be renewed.

Following that lead, states all over the nation began examining their banks and other corporations, and in just 1832, the state of Pennsylvania pulled the corporate charters of 10 corporations, sentencing them to corporate death "for operating contrary to the public interest."

Oil corporations, match manufacturers, whiskey trusts, and sugar corporations all received the corporate death penalty in the late 1800s in Michigan, Ohio, Nebraska, and New York, among others.

President Grover Cleveland invoked the mood of the times in his 1888 State of the Union address when he said,

> As we view the achievements of aggregated capital, we discover the existence of trusts, combinations, and monopolies, while the citizen is struggling far in the rear or is trampled to death beneath an iron heel. Corporations, which should be the carefully restrained creatures of the law and the servants of the people, are fast becoming the people's masters.[74]

Today, all of the states still have laws that allow them to impose the corporate death penalty; it's just been decades since these laws have been used against a large corporation. (Small companies are routinely shut down by secretaries of state, sometimes for malfeasance but mostly just because they've become inactive or failed to pay their taxes.)

Corporations have successfully argued before the Supreme Court that they should have First Amendment rights of free speech, Fourth Amendment rights of privacy, Fifth Amendment protections against takings, and 14th Amendment rights as "persons" to "equal protection [with you and me] under the law," among other "rights of personhood."

It's long past the time that these "persons," when they become egregious and recidivist criminals (and particularly when they repeatedly kill people), be treated the same as human criminals: remove them from society permanently. New, smaller, more innovative companies can fill the spaces now occupied by bloated corporate criminals. The result will be (as it was after AT&T was broken up in the 1970s for violating anti-monopoly laws) an explosion of innovation, competition, and opportunity.

If enough corporate criminals are targeted, the American business renaissance could spread across industries including media, pharma, airlines, tech, banking, insurance, food, chemicals, oil, and beyond.[75] It would be a *real* stimulus, meaningful and long-lasting: it's time for our states to start enforcing the corporate death penalty.

Solution: Ban Preemption Laws Written by Corporations

Preemption is a legal doctrine whereby superior government bodies may make rules that inferior (smaller) governments must follow or may not violate. A state, for example, can pass a law forbidding any of its towns or rural communities from banning fracking or giant hog farms.

Preemption essentially strips democracy away from communities; British preemption of colonial American laws is one of the main reasons why the Revolutionary War was fought and is heavily cited in the Declaration of Independence.

Federal preemption is why marijuana is still technically illegal in the states that have legalized it: it's still federally illegal, and federal agents can arrest you (as of this writing) even in states like Colorado and Oregon that have legalized it. The Constitution requires that federal law will almost always trump state laws: Article IV, Section 2, says that the Constitution and federal laws "shall be the supreme Law of the Land."

Where this doctrine goes off the rails is most often at the state level, where corporations can less expensively buy off legislators to ban counties, cities, or towns from regulating corporate harms to their citizens. States have passed preemption laws that forbid local communities from banning everything from fracking to giant hog farms and toxic waste plants. Preemption laws have been passed across the nation to prevent local control of the tobacco, pesticide, fossil fuel, nuclear, firearms, and pharmaceutical industries, among others.

The leading organization fighting against this corporate abuse of governmental powers is the Community Environmental Legal Defense Fund, which helps local folks draft laws that challenge preemption and work to restore local democracy.[76] CELDF's website is rich with their work in this area, and they also put on educational seminars and offer the help of their lawyers to communities under corporate assault.

While the US Supreme Court, most notably in *McCulloch v. Maryland* (1819) and *Pennsylvania v. Nelson* (1956), has extensively defined the powers and limits of federal preemption of state laws, the power of states to block local democracy hasn't been so well defined.

The golden era of state preemption laws began in 2010. In January of that election year, the US Supreme Court, in *Citizens United v. FEC*, overturned a century of good-government laws and ruled that virtually unlimited corporate (and billionaire) money could rain into the political process.

A few weeks later, in his State of the Union address, President Barack Obama said, "With all due deference to separation of powers, last week the Supreme Court reversed a century of law that I believe will open the floodgates for special interests—including foreign corporations—to spend without limit in our elections."

He was right, and, as in 1979 after the Supreme Court first legalized corporate bribery of politicians in its 1978 *First National Bank of Boston v. Bellotti* decision, the rest of 2010 and 2011 saw a geyser of corporate money flowing into state elections, with the GOP picking up 675 state legislative seats, nearly doubling their control of state legislatures (25, up from 14 in 2009), and seizing total control (House, Senate, governor) of fully 21 states.

Forty-three states have now passed laws forbidding cities from regulating gun ownership, 44 have passed laws prohibiting cities from regulating Uber or Lyft, 25 have blocked cities from raising their minimum wages, and 20 have made it illegal for a town or county to make low-cost high-speed internet service available to their citizens.[77]

Continuing the trend, in 2019, when the City Council of San Antonio, Texas, voted to kick Chick-fil-A out of their airport because of the company's anti-LGBTQ discriminatory hiring policies, the Texas Legislature passed a preemption law overturning the city's decision and banning any other city from doing the same. That year also saw the majority of preemption legislation submitted at the state level banning so-called sanctuary cities, guaranteeing a steady flow of cash to private prison contractors.[78]

While the real cancer here is a series of Supreme Court decisions, from *Buckley v. Valeo* to *Citizens United* to *McConnell v. FEC*, which need to be overturned (the subject of my book *The Hidden History of the Supreme Court and the Betrayal of America*), federal legislation to limit state preemption laws passed purely to benefit corporate interests is needed immediately.

The Core Solution: Competition

The key to a functioning regulated-capitalist economy is competition; as competition declines, so do innovation, investment, employment, and the wealth of working people. Lacking competition, those people and corporations in the economic top .01% will explode their wealth while everything and everybody else suffers.

Since the 1980s, when Reagan began aggressively applying Chicago School neoliberal policies and Robert Bork's perspective on antitrust, industry after industry, sector after sector, has been interpenetrated and then consumed almost entirely by cancer-like monopolies and oligopolies. Not only have wages and innovation suffered, but the overall economy itself has largely stagnated, relative to the preceding four decades.

As the Federal Reserve reports, the decade of the 1950s saw real GDP growth of 3.8%. Massive government infrastructure investment by Presidents Dwight D. Eisenhower, John F. Kennedy, and Lyndon B. Johnson, along with strict antitrust enforcement, saw GDP in the decade of the 1960s jump to 4.5%. The 1970s were hit by the shock of two Arab oil embargos producing a huge recession and double-digit inflation, but nonetheless they came in at 3.2%.[79]

Starting with Reagan's economic ideas, though, the next four decades went from 3.1% in the '80s to 3.0% in the '90s to 1.7% in the '00s to 2.1% in the 2010s.[80] And that's with several rounds of massive stimuli, a dropping of the top tax rate from 74% to around 28%, and the Fed lowering interest rates to ranges never seen before (creating a huge debt bubble that threatens, 1929 style, to wipe us out when it bursts).

Because these new monopolies and oligopolies that Reagan and his successors allowed to metastasize care more about protecting their markets than creating new products, America, once the world's leader in innovation and new patents, has now fallen behind China, which is growing its patent applications at a rate of over 14% annually while we've slipped to 0.2% growth.[81]

The grand neoliberal experiment of the Reagan Revolution, continued through the administrations of Bush, Clinton, Bush, Obama, and Trump, has failed. American consumers—who were supposed to be protected by Bork's insistence that low consumer prices were the only thing to consider with regard to antitrust laws—are paying more for cable TV, internet service, pharmaceuticals, air fares, health insurance, college, and imprisonment (among other things) than the residents of any other developed country in the world.

The cure for all this isn't some sort of big-government micromanagement of the economy; nor is it less antitrust regulation and thus even more consolidation to produce pure monopolies that are then regulated like utilities. Neither of these "solutions" will work over the long haul, although both have been tried at various times in various industries.

The cure for our cancer-ridden economy is to activate our economy's primary immune system: *competition*.

Competition, of course, is the result of specific rules being enforced, just like in sports. Twist the rules to benefit one side, and the game's no longer worth playing or watching.

When we deregulated much of our economy in the 1980s, knocking out the rules that allowed for a sportsperson-like competition among relative equals and killing off the spaces in which new companies could start and grow without being absorbed, the cancer of monopoly and oligopoly began to grow with a vengeance, as documented previously.

To bring back economic vitality, we must reject the now-discredited Bork doctrine and Reagan's neoliberalism and put back into place reasonable rules that support competition in the game of business.

That starts with Congress essentially reaffirming (and updating for the digital age) the 1890 Sherman Antitrust Act, the 1914 Clayton Antitrust Act, and the Celler-Kefauver Act of 1950 so that the Supreme Court will have to reverse its *GTE Sylvania* and subsequent rulings.

Nowhere in any of those laws do we find the phrase "consumer welfare"; instead, they all address the multiple harms caused across business, politics, and society itself by monopoly and its cousins. Bork's ideas must be revealed as utter failures, and we must return to sane antitrust policies.

We've been here before.

In the late 19th century, John D. Rockefeller grew a business cancer within the oil industry, Andrew Carnegie unleashed his business cancer in the steel industry, and J. P. Morgan metastasized his business throughout banking.

Others arose, each exploiting the cancerous tools of monopoly to freeze out competition and destroy competition: Cornelius Vanderbilt with railroads and steamboats (he died the richest man in the world); Éleuthère Irénée du Pont with gunpowder and chemicals; and a whole host of other monopolies within niche markets like manufacturing matches or train cars.

Some used vertical integration, like Carnegie and, in the early 20th century, Henry Ford, who owned everything necessary to make a car, from the iron mines to the ships and railroads to the plants that made steel and precision parts. Others monopolized horizontally, as Rockefeller did when he bought out or forced out of business virtually every oil company of consequence in several states where he operated.

Regardless of how the cancers of monopoly spread, Congress recognized this threat against our economic and political systems and passed the Sherman Antitrust Act to cure it. Progressive Republican Presidents Theodore Roosevelt and William Howard Taft used the law with enthusiasm, and Congress fine-tuned it with the Clayton Act and the Anti-Merger act, bringing us a half-century of prosperity.

Similarly, today's labor markets, lacking the immune system of unions, need to be cured by overturning the Taft-Hartley Act, which created the infamous "right to work for less" laws.

And we must address the shortsighted exploitation of the Earth's natural resources; the biosphere is the ultimate natural commons.

The economic disaster wrought on our nation by Donald Trump's feckless and incompetent handling of the coronavirus crisis presents us with new challenges as well as new opportunities.

All of these issues have been significantly exacerbated by the political power that corporations achieved through their monopoly and oligopoly status, and none will have a successful resolution without first breaking up these huge and concentrated sources of wealth and its attendant political power. As with Bork's transformation of America's business landscape, this healing process begins by understanding and publicizing the solution. Bork was an absolute evangelist for what he thought would positively change America's business landscape; now that we know he was wrong, we must become evangelists for a return to sanity.

A return to sanity means remembering that humans create the economy, and we should not be servants to our own creation.

A return to sanity means rejecting Bork's arguments that our governments, communities, and environment should be subordinate to low prices and high profits for investors.

It means forging a new framework for the game of business, where companies invest in our communities, respect and reinvest in their workers, and improve and protect our environment.

If we want our grandchildren and their grandchildren to have a chance at a vibrant democracy and a livable planet, we must bring back the corporate death penalty and break up the monopolistic corporate giants that are draining communities of their resources, impoverishing working people, and, in many cases, helping destroy the planet.

NOTES

Introduction: Cancer and Monopoly

1. https://www.nytimes.com/2019/11/10/opinion/big-business-consumer-prices.html
2. https://finance.yahoo.com/news/the-average-middleclass-family-in-the-us-is-spending-5000-more-a-year-than-it-should-economist-165256882.html
3. https://www.washingtonpost.com/nation/2019/09/11/ms-monopoly-female-inventor-lizzie-magie/
4. https://www.nytimes.com/1982/01/10/business/reagan-s-antitrust-explosion.html
5. https://www.vitacost.com/blog/food-nutrition/nutrition/how-is-soil-depletion-affecting-your-food.html
6. https://obamawhitehouse.archives.gov/blog/2011/12/06/archives-president-teddy-roosevelts-new-nationalism-speech
7. https://oll.libertyfund.org/quotes/367

Part One: America Was Founded on Resistance to Monopoly

1. I wrote far more extensively about this in my book *Unequal Protection: How Corporations Became "People"—and How You Can Fight Back* (San Francisco: Berrett-Koehler Publishers, 2010) and have used some of the text from that book in this chapter.
2. George R. T. Hewes, *A Retrospect of the Boston Tea-Party, With a Memoir of George R. T. Hewes, a Survivor of the Little Band of Patriots Who Drowned the Tea in Boston Harbour in 1773* (Franklin Classics, 2018).
3. Adam Smith, *An Inquiry into the Nature and Causes of the Wealth of Nations* (London: Strahan & Cadell, 1776).
4. Thomas Jefferson, *Delphi Complete Works of Thomas Jefferson* (Hastings, East Sussex, UK: Delphi Classics, 2019).
5. Jefferson, *Delphi Complete Works of Thomas Jefferson.*
6. Jefferson.
7. Jefferson.
8. Jefferson.
9. Jefferson.

10. Bill of Rights Institute, *Federalist Papers* No. 10, https://billofrightsinstitute.org/founding-documents/primary-source-documents/the-federalist-papers/federalist-papers-no-10/.

11. Alexandre Koyré, "An Unpublished Letter of Robert Hooke to Isaac Newton," *Isis* 43, no. 4 (December 1952), 312–37.

12. press-pubs.uchicago.edu/founders/documents/a1_8_8s12.html

13. Thomas Jefferson, letter to Isaac McPherson, written from New York, June 27, 1790 (from the author's collection).

14. Details are in Circular 15a, Duration of Copyright, and Circular 1, Copyright Basics, https://www.copyright.gov/circs/circ15a.pdf and https://www.copyright.gov/circs/circ01.pdf.

15. James Willard Hurst, *The Legitimacy of the Business Corporation in the Law of the United States 1780–1970* (Clark, NJ: Lawbook Exchange, 2004).

16. https://www.delawareinc.com/blog/new-delaware-companies-2017/

17. Wisconsin Laws, Section 4479a (Sec. I, ch. 492, 1905).

Part Two: Conservatives and Modern Monopolies vs. the Middle Class

1. https://www.theacp.org/2013/08/13/fusce-nec-odio-elit-in-interdum-velit/

2. https://www.jstor.org/stable/1805350?seq=1#page_scan_tab_contents

3. http://buzzflash.com/commentary/john-kenneth-galbraiths-the-great-crash-of-1929--thom-hartmanns-independent-thinker-review

4. https://equitablegrowth.org/u-s-income-inequality-persists-amid-overall-growth-2014/

5. http://drinkamerican.us/who-owns-what-beers/

6. https://www.cbinsights.com/research-top-food-and-beverage-brands

7. https://panam1901.org/visiting/salaries.htm

8. http://www.in2013dollars.com/us/inflation/1900?amount=449.80

9. http://jaysonlusk.com/blog/2016/6/26/the-evolution-of-american-agriculture

10. https://www.npr.org/2014/01/27/267145552/the-middle-class-took-off-100-years-ago-thanks-to-henry-ford

11. https://www.forbes.com/sites/timworstall/2012/03/04/the-story-of-henry-fords-5-a-day-wages-its-not-what-you-think/#3e9cbe7f766d

12. https://www2.census.gov/prod2/popscan/p60-039.pdf

13. https://www.census.gov/library/publications/1952/demo/p60-009.html

14. http://www.in2013dollars.com/us/inflation/1950?amount=3000

15. https://www.census.gov/library/publications/1971/demo/p60-78.html

16. https://www.epi.org/productivity-pay-gap/

17. https://www.usatoday.com/story/money/2019/04/17/these-ceos-make-1000-times-more-than-their-employees/39350499/

18. https://www.census.gov/content/dam/Census/library/publications/2017/acs/acsbr16-02.pdf

19. https://www.epi.org/productivity-pay-gap/

20. Ibid.

21. https://fred.stlouisfed.org/series/A053RC1Q027SBEA

22. https://www.bea.gov/data/gdp/gross-domestic-product; https://fred.stlouisfed.org/series/A053RC1Q027SBEA

23. http://www.industrialrevolution.org/10-hours-movement.html

24. Hansard House of Commons Debates vol. 60: cc100–2, 7 February 1842, https://api.parliament.uk/historic-hansard/commons/1842/feb/07/poor-law-factory-regulations

25. https://millercenter.org/the-presidency/presidential-speeches/may-19-1869-proclamation-establishing-eight-hour-workday

26. Richard Borshay Lee, *The !Kung San: Men, Women, and Work in a Foraging Society* (Cambridge, UK: Cambridge University Press, 1979).

27. Marshall Sahlins, *Stone Age Economics* (Aldine Press, 1994).

28. I wrote far more extensively about this in my book *The Crash of 2016* (Twelve Books, 2014, out of print), and have used some of the text of that book, updated and revised, in this chapter.

29. http://content.time.com/time/magazine/article/0,9171,835128,00.html

30. https://www.washingtonpost.com/business/2019/10/08/first-time-history-us-billionaires-paid-lower-tax-rate-than-working-class-last-year/

31. http://piketty.pse.ens.fr/files/Scheidel2009.pdf

32. A facsimile is shown here: https://scholarlycommons.law.wlu.edu/cgi/viewcontent.cgi?article=1000&context=powellmemo

33. Jack Anderson, "Powell's Lesson to Business Aired," *Washington Post*, September 28, 1972.

34. Ibid.

35. Ibid.

36. ReclaimDemocracy.org, "The Powell Memo," http://reclaimdemocracy.org/powell_memo_lewis/
37. Ibid.
38. Ibid.
39. Ibid.
40. Ibid.
41. Ibid.
42. Ibid.
43. Ibid.
44. https://www.publicpower.org/public-power
45. https://www.wsj.com/articles/pg-e-knew-for-years-its-lines-could-spark-wildfires-and-didnt-fix-them-11562768885
46. https://www.kqed.org/news/11737336/judge-pge-paid-out-stock-dividends-instead-of-trimming-trees
47. https://www.sfgate.com/bayarea/article/pge-underground-power-lines-cost-14503808.php
48. https://www.scientificamerican.com/article/analysis-clouds-over-hawaiis-roofto/
49. Ibid.
50. https://www.tni.org/files/publication-downloads/reclaiming_public_services.pdf
51. Thomas J. DiLorenzo, "The Myth of Natural Monopoly," *Review of Austrian Economics* 9, no. 2 (1999), https://mises.org/library/myth-natural-monopoly-0
52. Mark Ames, "When Congress Busted Milton Friedman (and Libertarianism Was Created by Big Business Lobbyists)," NSFWCorp, November 16, 2012, https://www.nsfwcorp.com/dispatch/milton-friedman/
53. Ibid.
54. https://www.theguardian.com/commentisfree/2019/nov/22/surprised-about-mark-zuckerbergs-secret-meeting-with-trump-dont-be
55. I wrote far more extensively about this in my book *Screwed: The Undeclared War on the Middle Class* (San Francisco: Berrett-Koehler Publishers, 2007) and have used some of the text of that book in this chapter.
56. Marc Bloch, *Feudal Society*, trans. L. A. Manyon (Chicago: University of Chicago Press, 1961).
57. Ibid.

58. Ibid.
59. https://ips-dc.org/billionaire-bonanza/
60. https://www.forbes.com/sites/luisakroll/2017/10/17/forbes-400-2017-americas-richest-people-bill-gates-jeff-bezos-mark-zuckerberg-donald-trump/#3d844895ed53
61. John C. Weicher, "The Distribution of Wealth in America, 1983–2013," Hudson Institute, January 31, 2017, https://www.hudson.org/research/13095-the-distribution-of-wealth-in-america-1983-2013
62. https://www.usinflationcalculator.com
63. https://www.census.gov/const/uspricemon.pdf
64. https://www.ey.com/en_us/public-policy/what-is-behind-the-decline-in-public-companies
65. Jonathan Tepper, *The Myth of Capitalism: Monopolies and the Death of Competition* (Hoboken, NJ: John Wiley & Sons, 2019).
66. http://www.janeeckhout.com/wp-content/uploads/RMP.pdf
67. https://www.ncbi.nlm.nih.gov/pmc/articles/PMC6170097/
68. Barak Orbach, "Was the Crisis in Antitrust a Trojan Horse?" *Antitrust Law Journal* 79, no. 3 (2014), https://orbach.org
69. Brian Doherty, "The Economist and the Dictator: Just What Is the Connection Between Milton Friedman and Augusto Pinochet?" *Reason*, December 15, 2006, https://reason.com/archives/2006/12/15/the-economist-and-the-dictator
70. https://www.commondreams.org/views/2018/10/27/neoliberalism-and-fascism-stealth-connection
71. https://digitalcommons.law.yale.edu/cgi/viewcontent.cgi?article=5243&context=fss_papers
72. https://www.statista.com/statistics/828283/market-share-of-footwear-brands-us/
73. https://supreme.justia.com/cases/federal/us/433/36/
74. https://papers.ssrn.com/sol3/papers.cfm?abstract_id=2327364
75. https://www.forbes.com/sites/angelauyeung/2019/08/01/mackenzie-bezos-now-officially-worlds-third-richest-woman/#a7090aa4d81f

Part Three: Living Monopoly Today and in Praise of Inefficiency

1. https://www.youtube.com/watch?v=XEI6HbCZjRQ
2. https://www.publicopiniononline.com/story/news/2018/03/12/milk-processor-cancels-farm-contracts-walmart-makes-own-milk/417995002/

3. https://www.farmprogress.com/dairy/michigan-dairy-farmers-either-exit-or-eat-equity

4. https://www.chicagotribune.com/g00/business/ct-biz-winn-dixie-tyson-chicken-prices-20180115-story.html?i10c.encReferrer=

5. https://www.huffpost.com/entry/bernie-sanders-agribusiness_n_5cb0a662e4b0ffefe3afba70

6. http://www.genfkd.org/monopoly-on-insulin

7. https://globenewswire.com/news-release/2018/11/19/1653404/0/en/Human-Insulin-Market-to-Reach-70-6-billion-by-2023-P-S-Intelligence.html

8. Ibid.

9. https://www.washingtonpost.com/news/wonk/wp/2016/10/31/why-insulin-prices-have-kept-rising-for-95-years/?noredirect=on&utm_term=.a98f39f461e7

10. https://prospect.org/article/beyond-planet-pharma-bros

11. Ibid.

12. https://www.nytimes.com/2016/02/21/opinion/sunday/break-up-the-insulin-racket.html

13. https://www.ncci.com/Articles/Pages/II_Insights_QEB_Impact-of-Hospital-Consolidation-on-Medical-Costs.aspx

14. https://www.theguardian.com/us-news/2019/dec/27/missouri-twin-rivers-hospital-medical-center-healthcare-crisis-america-dying

15. https://www.pbs.org/independentlens/democracyondeadline/mediaownership.html

16. https://www.theverge.com/2019/8/8/20758905/iheartmedia-podcast-sundays-radio-stations

17. https://www.politico.com/story/2011/06/top-radio-talkers-sell-endorsements-056997

18. https://www.washingtonpost.com/wp-dyn/content/article/2006/05/03/AR2006050302299.html

19. https://s3.amazonaws.com/s3.boldprogressives.org/images/Big_Ideas-Polling_PDF-1.pdf; http://www.gbaostrategies.com/clients/

20. https://www.theguardian.com/us-news/2017/oct/19/big-pharma-money-lobbying-us-opioid-crisis

21. http://www.pnhp.org/excessdeaths/health-insurance-and-mortality-in-US-adults.pdf

22. https://www.nytimes.com/2010/02/05/us/politics/05loans.html

23. https://www.wsj.com/articles/colleges-flex-lobbying-muscle-1447037474

24. http://pnhp.org/news/new-poll-on-single-payer-and-a-medicare-buy-in/; https://www.opensecrets.org/lobby/indusclient.php?id=F09&year=2018; https://www.forbes.com/sites/brucejapsen/2019/08/04/as-sanders-and-warren-attack-private-health-insurer-profits-soar/#6eb5c14c532b

25. https://s3.amazonaws.com/s3.boldprogressives.org/images/Big_Ideas-Polling_PDF-1.pdf

26. https://www.businessinsider.com/millennials-americans-worry-about-kids-children-climate-change-poll-2019-3

27. http://priceofoil.org/content/uploads/2017/10/OCI_US-Fossil-Fuel-Subs-2015-16_Final_Oct2017.pdf

28. https://www.nydailynews.com/news/national/ny-vaping-lung-disease-death-toll-centers-for-disease-control-20190913-kqzio5wp5rd4xempv7ktwze7wy-story.html; https://www.resilience.org/stories/2019-02-20/revealed-how-the-tobacco-and-fossil-fuel-industries-fund-disinformation-campaigns-around-the-world/

29. https://www.ctpost.com/news/article/Wendy-Lecker-Charter-lobby-still-paying-for-13508624.php

30. https://www.washingtonpost.com/posteverything/wp/2015/04/28/how-for-profit-prisons-have-become-the-biggest-lobby-no-one-is-talking-about/

31. https://www.nytimes.com/interactive/2019/climate/trump-environment-rollbacks.html

32. https://www.nytimes.com/2018/02/02/us/politics/payday-lenders-lobbying-regulations.html

33. https://www.amazon.com/Hidden-History-Second-Amendment-Hartmann/dp/1523085991/

34. https://www.politifact.com/truth-o-meter/statements/2016/jan/13/barack-obama/obama-us-spends-more-military-next-8-nations-combi/

35. https://www.amazon.com/History-Supreme-Betrayal-America-Hartmann/dp/1523085940/

36. https://www.amazon.com/Unequal-Protection-Corporations-Became-People/dp/1605095591/

37. https://www.cambridge.org/core/journals/perspectives-on-politics/article/testing-theories-of-american-politics-elites-interest-groups-and-average-citizens/62327F513959D0A304D489 3B382B992B

39. https://www.washingtonpost.com/politics/2019/09/12/september-democratic-debate-abc-univision-houston/

40. https://movetoamend.org/

41. https://www.revolutionary-war-and-beyond.com/property-by-james-madison-march-29-1792.html

42. https://www.theguardian.com/inequality/2017/sep/13/median-wealth-of-black-americans-will-fall-to-zero-by-2053-warns-new-report

43. Ibid.

44. https://www.cnn.com/2014/08/07/living/sixties-women-5-things/

45. Ibid.

46. https://www.law.cornell.edu/supremecourt/text/381/479

47. https://www.cnn.com/2014/08/07/living/sixties-women-5-things/

48. https://www.census.gov/quickfacts/fact/table/US/PST045218

49. https://www.nytimes.com/interactive/2017/09/18/upshot/black-white-wealth-gap-perceptions.html

50. https://www.filmsforaction.org/articles/defeat-the-right-in-three-minutes/

51. https://www.equalitytrust.org.uk is the website; their two books are *Why Inequality Matters* and *The Spirit Level*.

52. https://hrdailyadvisor.blr.com/2014/09/02/monkeys-and-dogs-react-to-workplace-unfairness/ and https://www.npr.org/templates/story/story.php?storyId=97944783

53. https://papers.ssrn.com/sol3/papers.cfm?abstract_id=2769132

54. https://www.washingtonpost.com/opinions/how-america-became-uncompetitive-and-unequal/2014/06/13/a690ad94-ec00-11e3-b98c-72cef4a00499_story.html

55. https://www.epi.org/publication/ceo-compensation-2018/

56. https://www.wsj.com/articles/SB119697535545316199

57. http://www.startribune.com/ceo-pay-watch-stephen-hemsley-unitedhealth-group-executive-chairman/480423243/

58. https://www.marketwatch.com/story/40-of-americans-struggle-to-pay-for-one-basic-need-like-food-housing-or-health-care-2018-08-28

59. https://www.forbes.com/sites/joshbersin/2018/10/31/
    why-arent-wages-keeping-up-its-not-the-economy-its-
    management/#3bd3dcaf397e
60. https://www.youtube.com/watch?v=welnY4LiEfk
61. https://www.youtube.com/watch?v=79qXC5P4cSE
62. https://www.saleminternational.org/index.php?seite=en-index
63. http://www.victorianweb.org/art/architecture/clubs/black.html
64. https://www.gilderlehrman.org/history-now/journals/2008-09/
    theodore-roosevelt-and-progressive-era
65. http://www-personal.umd.umich.edu/~ppennock/Progressive%20
    Reforms.htm
66. https://www.forbes.com/profile/mark-zuckerberg/#63cb14543e06
67. https://allthingsliberty.com/2014/02/you-wont-believe-how-
    samuel-adams-recruited-sons-of-liberty/
68. http://www.americanradioworks.org/segments/radio-the-
    internet-of-the-1930s/
69. https://www.newsweek.com/facebook-google-internet-traffic-net-
    neutrality-monopoly-699286
70. https://www.cnbc.com/2019/09/03/senator-wyden-prison-for-
    facebook-ceo-zuckerberg-should-be-considered.html
71. https://theweek.com/articles/582042/why-should-just-
    nationalize-facebook
72. https://books.google.com/books?id=ALX3iCND6ekC&pg=
    PA249#v=onepage&q&f=false
73. https://books.google.com/books?id=BzdOAQAAIAAJ&pg=
    PA17#v=onepage&q&f=false
74. https://en.wikisource.org/wiki/Grover_Cleveland%27s_Fourth_
    State_of_the_Union_Address
75. http://lib.law.virginia.edu/Garrett/corporate-prosecution-registry/
    browse/browse.html
76. https://celdf.org
77. https://www.citylab.com/equity/2019/08/states-gun-control-
    cities-preemption-laws-legislation/595759/
78. Ibid.
79. https://www.federalreserve.gov/newsevents/speech/files/
    powell20190823a.pdf
80. https://www.bloomberg.com/opinion/articles/2018-01-18/low-
    economic-volatility-won-t-keep-markets-calm-forever
81. https://www.wipo.int/pressroom/en/articles/2018/article_0012

ACKNOWLEDGMENTS

Special thanks go to Troy N. Miller, who worked with me for years as a producer and writer for the television show *The Big Picture*, which I hosted every weeknight for seven years in Washington, DC. Troy worked hard as a researcher, sounding board, editor, and often cowriter on parts of this book, and deserves recognition for it.

At Berrett-Koehler Publishers, Steve Piersanti—who was the founder—worked with me to kick off this series. It's been a labor of love for both of us, and I'm so grateful to Steve for his insights, rigor, and passion for this project. Of the many other people at BK who have helped with this book (and some projects associated with it), special thanks to Jeevan Sivasubramaniam (who has helped keep me sane for years) and Neal Maillet. BK is an extraordinary publishing company, and it's been an honor to have them publish my books for almost two decades. And thanks to Tai Moses, who edited my *Thom Hartmann Reader* and returned to do a first pass with this book, for all her insights and help.

BK also provided a brilliant final editor for the book, Elissa Rabellino, who did a great job smoothing and tightening the text.

Bill Gladstone, my agent for over two decades, helped make this book—and the *Hidden History* series—possible. Bill is truly one of the best in the business.

My executive producer, Shawn Taylor, helped with booking expert guests on my radio and TV programs, many of whom provided great information and anecdotes for this book. And my video producer, Nate Atwell, is a true visual genius. I'm blessed to have such a great team helping me produce a daily radio and TV program, which supports my writing work.

And, as always, my best sounding board, editor, and friend is my wife, Louise. Without her, in all probability none of my books would ever have seen the light of day.

INDEX

ABOUT THE AUTHOR

© Ian Sbalcio

Thom Hartmann is the four-time Project Censored Award–winning, *New York Times* best-selling author of more than 25 books currently in print in over a dozen languages on five continents in the fields of psychiatry, ecology, politics, and economics, and the number one progressive-talk-show host in the United States.

His daily three-hour radio/TV show is syndicated on commercial radio stations nationwide, on nonprofit and community stations nationwide and in Europe and Africa by Pacifica, across the entire North American continent on SiriusXM Satellite Radio, on its own YouTube channel, via podcast, on Facebook Live, worldwide through the US American Forces Network, and through the Thom Hartmann app in the App Store and for Android. The show is also simulcast as TV in real time into over 60 million US homes by the Free Speech TV network on Dish Network, DirecTV, and cable TV systems nationwide.

He has helped set up hospitals, famine relief programs, schools, and refugee centers in India, Uganda, Australia, Colombia, Russia, Israel, and the United States. Formerly rostered with the state of Vermont as a psychotherapist, founder of the Michigan Healing Arts Center, and licensed as an NLP Trainer by Richard Bandler, he was the originator of the

revolutionary Hunter/Farmer Hypothesis to understand attention deficit hyperactivity disorder (ADHD).

In the field of environmentalism, Thom has cowritten and
costarred in four documentaries with Leonardo DiCaprio,
and is also featured in his documentary theatrical releases *The
11th Hour* and *Ice on Fire*. His book *The Last Hours of Ancient
Sunlight*, about the end of the age of oil and the inspiration
for *The 11th Hour*, is an international best seller and used as a
textbook in many schools.

Thom lives with his wife of 48 years, Louise, and their two
dogs and three cats, on the Columbia River in Portland, Oregon. They're the parents of three adult children.

BOOKS BY THOM HARTMANN

Also in the Hidden History Series

The Hidden History of Guns and the Second Amendment

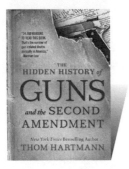

Thom Hartmann, the most popular progressive radio host in America and a *New York Times* bestselling author, reveals the real history of guns in America and what we can do to limit both their lethal impact and the power of the gun lobby. Taking an in-depth, historically informed view, Hartmann examines the brutal role guns have played in American history, from the genocide of the Native Americans to the enforcement of slavery and post–Civil War racism, coining the term "the Unholy Trinity of racism, genocide, and guns." He also exposes the alliance of the NRA and conservative Supreme Court justices that invented the unlimited right to own guns. Ever practical, Hartmann identifies solutions that can break the power of the gun lobby and put an end to the alarming reality of gun violence in the United States.

Paperback, 192 pages, ISBN 978-1-5230-8599-6
PDF ebook, ISBN 978-1-5230-8600-9
ePub ebook, ISBN 978-1-5230-8601-6
Digital audio, ISBN 978-1-5230-8603-0

BK Berrett–Koehler Publishers, Inc.
www.bkconnection.com   **800.929.2929**

Also in the Hidden History Series

The Hidden History of the Supreme Court and the Betrayal of America

This volume of Thom Hartmann's explosive series of hidden histories critiques the omnipotent Supreme Court and offers pathways toward returning power to the people. Taking his typically in-depth, historically informed view, Hartmann asks, What if the Supreme Court didn't have the power to strike down laws? According to the Constitution, it doesn't. From the founding of the republic until 1803, the Supreme Court was the final court of appeals, as it was always meant to be. The role of deciding what the law is belongs not to the Supreme Court but to the people themselves, who vote at the ballot box. America does not belong to the kings and queens of the Court, it belongs to us.

Paperback, 192 pages, ISBN 978-1-5230-8594-1
PDF ebook, ISBN 978-1-5230-8596-5
ePub ebook, ISBN 978-1-5230-8597-2
Digital audio, ISBN 978-1-5230-8595-8

BK Berrett–Koehler Publishers, Inc.
www.bkconnection.com   800.929.2929

Also in the Hidden History Series

The Hidden History of the War on Voting

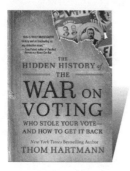

In today's America, only a slim majority of people register to vote, and a large percentage of registered voters don't bother to show up: Donald Trump was elected by only 26 percent of eligible voters. Unfortunately, this is not a bug in our system, it's a feature. Thom Hartmann unveils the strategies and tactics that conservative elites in this country have used, from the foundation of the Electoral College to the latest voter ID laws, to protect their interests by preventing "the wrong people"—such as the poor, women, and people of color—from voting while making it more convenient for the wealthy and white. But he also lays out a wide variety of simple, commonsense ways that we the people can fight back and reclaim our right to rule through the ballot box.

Paperback, 192 pages, ISBN 978-1-5230-8778-5
PDF ebook, ISBN 978-1-5230-8779-2
ePub ebook, ISBN 978-1-5230-8780-8
Digital audio, ISBN 978-1-5230-8781-5

Berrett–Koehler Publishers, Inc.
www.bkconnection.com

800.929.2929

Berrett–Koehler
Publishers

Berrett-Koehler is an independent publisher dedicated to an ambitious mission: *Connecting people and ideas to create a world that works for all.*

Our publications span many formats, including print, digital, audio, and video. We also offer online resources, training, and gatherings. And we will continue expanding our products and services to advance our mission.

We believe that the solutions to the world's problems will come from all of us, working at all levels: in our society, in our organizations, and in our own lives. Our publications and resources offer pathways to creating a more just, equitable, and sustainable society. They help people make their organizations more humane, democratic, diverse, and effective (and we don't think there's any contradiction there). And they guide people in creating positive change in their own lives and aligning their personal practices with their aspirations for a better world.

And we strive to practice what we preach through what we call "The BK Way." At the core of this approach is *stewardship,* a deep sense of responsibility to administer the company for the benefit of all of our stakeholder groups, including authors, customers, employees, investors, service providers, sales partners, and the communities and environment around us. Everything we do is built around stewardship and our other core values of *quality, partnership, inclusion,* and *sustainability.*

This is why Berrett-Koehler is the first book publishing company to be both a B Corporation (a rigorous certification) and a benefit corporation (a for-profit legal status), which together require us to adhere to the highest standards for corporate, social, and environmental performance. And it is why we have instituted many pioneering practices (which you can learn about at www.bkconnection.com), including the Berrett-Koehler Constitution, the Bill of Rights and Responsibilities for BK Authors, and our unique Author Days.

We are grateful to our readers, authors, and other friends who are supporting our mission. We ask you to share with us examples of how BK publications and resources are making a difference in your lives, organizations, and communities at www.bkconnection.com/impact.

Dear reader,

Thank you for picking up this book and welcome to the worldwide BK community! You're joining a special group of people who have come together to create positive change in their lives, organizations, and communities.

What's BK all about?

Our mission is to connect people and ideas to create a world that works for all.

Why? Our communities, organizations, and lives get bogged down by old paradigms of self-interest, exclusion, hierarchy, and privilege. But we believe that can change. That's why we seek the leading experts on these challenges—and share their actionable ideas with you.

A welcome gift

To help you get started, we'd like to offer you a free copy of one of our bestselling ebooks:

www.bkconnection.com/welcome

When you claim your **free ebook,** you'll also be subscribed to our blog.

Our freshest insights

Access the best new tools and ideas for leaders at all levels on our blog at ideas.bkconnection.com.

Sincerely,

Your friends at Berrett-Koehler